Be a Kickass Assistant

How to Get from a Grunt Job to a Great Career

Heather Beckel

WARNER BOOKS

An AOL Time Warner Company

Warner Books, Inc., 1271 Avenue of the Americas, New York, NY 10020

Visit our Web site at www.twbookmark.com.

 An AOL Time Warner Company

Printed in the United States of America

First Printing: May 2002

10 9 8 7 6 5 4 3 2 1

Library of Congress Cataloging-in-Publication Data

Beckel, Heather.
   Be a kickass assistant: how to get from a grunt job to a great career/Heather Beckel.
       p. cm.
   Includes index.
   ISBN 0-446-67814-7
       1. Managing your boss. 2. Career development. I. Title

Hf5547.5 .B398/ 2001
650.1'13—dc21

2001026872

Book design by Nancy Singer Olaguera
Cover design by Brigid Pearson
Cover illustration by Paul Gilligan

In memory of my father,
Edwin Reid Beckel

acknowledgments

First and foremost, I want to thank George Stephanopoulos for giving me what is still the coolest job I've ever had. He has never failed to stand by me and offer his help both as a boss and as a friend. George set a high standard for me when I was young and I continue to strive to reach his level of excellence.

Thank you to Wendy Smith for conceiving that such a book was needed and encouraging me to write it. Thank you to my agent, Margaret McBride, and her wonderful staff, particularly Sangeeta Mehta and Kris Wallace. Thank you to my editor, Molly Chehak, who is really good at her job and who made this book much better.

Thank you to my mother for her continued support and friendship, without which I never could have volunteered on the Clinton Campaign in 1991, or written this book in 2001. Thank you to Jason Guntert, who always tells me that everything's going to be okay, and I believe him. Thank you to my good friend, Roberto Rojas, for being such a great manager and allowing me to leave my restaurant in his capable hands to write this book. Thank you also to: Lisa Carlson, Virginia Cox, Dennis Harmon, Bartley Johnstone, Emily Lenzner, Calvin

Mitchell, Nina Plank, Anne Reingold, Jill Savitt, and Martha Swiller for their friendship, love, and support, and for all the ideas and information they offered.

Finally, I want to thank my brother, Jeff Beckel, who was unbelievably generous with his time and love. He was this book's first editor, and never failed to give me whatever I needed in encouragement, ideas, stories, and even computer tech support.

Be a
Kickass
Assistant

The Best Cup of Coffee They'll Ever Taste

This book is for anyone who has found their way to the city of his or her choice and into the industry of their dreams. Once you get there, you'll probably find that your first job will be as the assistant to an executive. Unfortunately, you'll find that what you learned in college isn't much use and the company you work for doesn't offer a training program in how to be a kickass assistant. If you are smart and ambitious and want to excel at your new job as an assistant, then this book is for you.

Why Be an Assistant?

Being an assistant is a great first job. It helps to be in a good company and to have a good boss. But even without these advantages, if you work very hard, you'll learn a lot and develop a strong foundation for your future career. The skills necessary to be a good assistant will serve you throughout your professional career: organization, diplomacy, problem solving, prioritizing, time management, and communication. Many of these skills are exactly what is needed for certain jobs; for example, entry-level public relations jobs are no more than coordination and administrative work. As an assistant, you'll have the opportunity to:

- Impress senior-level executives at your own and other companies
- Learn what it takes to become an executive
- Learn how the company works

As an assistant to an executive you'll have access to other executives that you wouldn't have in another entry-level position because they'll be dealing with you to get to your boss. They'll know who you are, and you'll have a chance to impress them with your performance. You'll be an apprentice to your boss in that you'll learn what it takes to be an executive. You can learn how he does his job, and judge what he does that you admire and what you'd do differently. You'll have more of a chance to learn about the overall goals of the company than you'd have in another junior-level position from which you'd have a very narrow view of the company. You'll learn about the different departments within your company and about different companies within your industry, and through this you'll gain a greater understanding of your own career goals. As long as your chosen industry is not in one of the professional fields (law, medicine, engineering), which require a specific college degree, a position as an assistant can be a stepping stone, and with a little fair play from your boss and a lot of hard work from you, your boss will help you move on to the next job of your choice. Another reason to learn to be a great assistant is that at your next job, you'll most likely have to be your own assistant—and you'll want to be a good one. You'll answer your own phone and mail, and you'll keep your own schedule. And when you do get to hire your own assistant, chances are you'll have to train him to be a great assistant.

Why Read This Book?

The goal of this book is to teach you how to be a great assistant. Get a pen and make notes in this book because it is designed to be a tool. There are specific instructions on how to do everything necessary to succeed, from getting the most out of your first day to your final day of departure from the job. I'll walk you through communicating with your boss and organizing his time; I'll teach you how to take the job to the next level, which will make you indispensable; and I'll tell you how to get through all of the dull but necessary work. I'll teach you everything you need—everything except how to work very hard. I'm writing this assuming that you're ambitious and that you either want to use this first job as a springboard to your next great opportunity or that you want to build a career as a corporate executive assistant. Either way, working very hard is a prerequisite for success. If you're not interested in getting in early and staying late, or if you took a job as an assistant because you thought you could talk to your friends on the phone and surf the net all day—forget it. Every great assistant works as hard—or harder—than anyone else in the company. The working world is very competitive, and if you're in an enviable job, in a prestigious industry, in a major city, there will be plenty of young people just like you who want your job. When people talk about the drive and ambition needed to succeed, they're talking about a willingness to give up everything else in their life for their job, making work their number-one priority. This means getting in early, staying late, working on weekends, and always being willing to give up your plans in the evening to stay at work when necessary. The good news is that if you're willing to work this hard, you'll succeed because most employees at a company or organization are very mediocre. Most people don't work hard and aren't smart about what they're doing. Most people are too lazy to read this book and learn how to be great at their job.

I was an assistant for three and a half years and it was the best professional experience of my life. That is not to say that it was always fun, or even interesting, but it was the best foundation for every other position I've held since. I didn't set out to be an assistant. I was in my mid-twenties and had just returned from living in Italy for two years. I was living in my parents' basement in Little Rock, Arkansas, while I halfheartedly studied for the GRE, planning to go to graduate school. My mother encouraged me to volunteer on the primary campaign of Governor Bill Clinton just to get out of the house for a few hours every day. I went down to the campaign headquarters in October 1991 and volunteered my time. It was early in the campaign. There were only a few paid staff members and I was passed around between them doing odd jobs. The wife of campaign manager David Wilhelm, Degee, was answering the deputy campaign manager's phone. Luckily for me, she was destined for greater things. (She went on to be Governor Clinton's traveling aide and personal assistant.) The minute I sat at her desk, I knew it was where I wanted to spend the rest of the campaign. I was in awe of the deputy campaign manager, George Stephanopoulos, and even then I knew I was lucky to be in the room with him. When George, with his characteristic low-key manner, told me he was moving me from a volunteer to a paid position as his assistant, with a beer in his hand at the Clintons' Holiday Party at the Governor's Mansion in 1991, I was elated.

The day after Election Day in 1992, George and I moved offices to the Presidential Transition headquarters in Little Rock. The Presidential Transition is the period from Election Day (the first week of November) until Inauguration Day (January 20) when the new president-elect prepares to move to the White House, and the outgoing president prepares to move out. For me, it was the worst possible time; all of our friends from the campaign were out of work, and everyone was scrambling for a position in the new administration. Résumés were showing up in our office by the hundreds every day. The desperation was best illustrated by the determined individual who slid her résumé under the door of the toilet stall where press secretary Dee Dee Myers was a captive audience. One day, George came back from a meeting with President-Elect Clinton and chief of staff to-be, Mack McLarty, and told me, with barely contained euphoria, that they'd offered him an appointment as White House Communications Director. In the same conversation, he offered me a position as his assistant there, and understandably expected the same excitement from me. But I was too naïve to understand what George was offering me. I'd been working with George sixteen- to eighteen-hour days for fourteen months, and I was exhausted. After the disillusioning weeks of the transition, I was no longer motivated by the challenge and fun of my job. I asked him if I could think it over for a few days.

Looking back, George could not have been a better friend and mentor. But his impatience with my ignorance showed through when he said that, sure, I could think over the offer, but told me I had no idea of the scope of what this meant, and that I'd be crazy not to go to Washington. Thankfully, my trust and respect for George kicked in, and I accepted his offer on the spot. Never underestimate what can be in store for you when you take a chance.

Are You a Natural?

I learned how to be a great assistant on the job. I was fortunate to have a boss who had never had an assistant, and he grew into the role of boss as I grew into my role as his assistant. Also to my advantage was my experience working on a campaign. A campaign, unlike a corporation, has a very loose atmosphere, and the priority is to get the job done any way you can. The job of assistant came naturally to me; I'm very organized, efficient, and compulsive. I also have a good memory and like taking care of people; thus managing someone's life comes easily to me. I wrote this book because I know the ability to manage the details of someone else's life doesn't come easily to everyone, and certainly few people will get the break I did in having such a forgiving working environment. If being an assistant doesn't come naturally to you, if you aren't naturally organized and efficient, don't worry; I'll teach you how to learn all the skills you need to be a kickass assistant.

Assistant Versus Secretary

Technology has been a godsend to assistants because as new generations of computer-literate employees come up through the ranks and get assistants, they don't need their assistants to type for them. Many are even comfortable faxing documents from their computers, and of course, talking to associates via e-mail. All of this frees up assistants to do other, more interesting work. You may have an older or more conservative boss who is unable or unwilling to take on some tasks, but if you're an assistant, it is unlikely that you'll have a boss who expects you to take dictation and type all his documents. The image of a woman taking dictation from a male boss makes us all think of a secretary, and while there might still be a role for traditional secretaries in some industries and companies, you're not a secretary.

The title of secretary is too tainted by clichéd perceptions (including sexism) to be fair in today's workplace, and the limited position of a secretary is out of date in modern industry where everyone is expected to be smarter and take on more responsibility. Every decade the bar is set higher for the educational and training standards of employees. Thirty years ago a bachelor's degree was a big deal, but now it is as standard as a high school diploma in professional settings. And with the trend toward downsizing in successful businesses, there's less and less room for employees with limited skills who are unable (or unwilling) to take on added responsibilities. The distinction between secretary and assistant is hard for some people to grasp, mostly people who've never been an assistant. Thankfully the workplace has become less sexist and more egalitarian, and today, most young bosses, both male and female, were once someone's assistants. In fact, all the women (and many of the men) I interviewed for this book had been assistants at one time, and they're concerned today that their assistants have a positive learning experience. However, if you're a woman, you'll probably have the unpleasant experience of being treated as, or even called, a secretary by someone. At the White House, Clinton's first chief of staff, Mack McLarty, once introduced me to Lee

Iacocca (the former chairman of Chrysler) as George's secretary. Mack is a true gentleman, and he was treating me with respect by bothering to introduce me to Iacocca at all (I was escorting him through the White House), however, my cheeks burned at the word secretary. I felt demeaned and angry. I knew that Mack would never introduce press secretary Dee Dee Myers's male assistant as her "secretary," but the experience tells more about Mack, and his age and bias, than about my value as George's assistant. Sexism is still prevalent, especially for female assistants.

My friend Lucy worked as the assistant to a member of congress, and while the congressman was traveling with his chief of staff, the chief of staff remembered his wedding anniversary. He called the office desperately needing someone to send flowers to his wife, but instead of asking a friend in the office to do him this personal favor, which had nothing to do with the congressional office, he asked Lucy. The appropriate thing to do is to ask a friend. The same chief of staff also asked the congressman's (female) scheduler to sew a button back onto his jacket. The only way to handle these situations is to set boundaries. Do the favor for the person who is not your boss, as long as it will not take up too much of your time. When you tell him the task is done, let him know that you did it as a personal favor and that you do personal errands for your boss only. Say: "John, I made your dinner reservation at Chez Martin for tonight at 7:30. Listen, I didn't mind doing this personal favor for you because I had a few minutes to spare, but normally I can't take time away from my job as George's assistant to help you out with personal errands. I'm sure you understand." Don't get angry or defensive. If the problem persists, or if you're too scared to confront the person taking advantage of your time, ask your boss for help. Explain to your boss that these tasks are beyond your job description, and that doing personal tasks for another person cuts into your time working for him. This makes it in his best interest to deal with the situation.

Secretary	Assistant
"One employed to handle correspondence and manage routine and detail work for superior" *(Merriam-Webster's Tenth Edition)*	"A person who assists" *(Merriam-Webster's Tenth Edition)*
Old-fashioned	Modern
Professional career	Stepping stone to a promotion
Female	Female or male
Clerical	Clerical and everything else
Works 9–5	Works 24 hours a day, as needed
Bound by role	Works in a meritocracy
High school diploma	College degree (probably liberal arts)
Doesn't have partnership with boss	Has a partnership with boss
Limited access to information	Access to information
Boss doesn't ask for her opinion	Opinion is asked for and given
Limited responsibilities	Responsibilities only limited by ambition
Chance of promotion out of secretary role is slim	Chance of promotion out of assistant role is huge

Some Great Advice

I received the two most important pieces of professional advice I've ever been given in my first weeks on the '92 Clinton for President campaign. This advice has served me well in every job I've had since. Steve (Scoop) Cohen, another staffer fresh out of college, told me that when someone asked him for a cup of coffee he didn't waste a second worrying about the demeaning act of serving coffee. He brought him the best cup of coffee he'd ever tasted as fast as possible. He didn't ask if he wanted sugar or milk—he brought both with a stirrer and a napkin. The point is to take every advantage to impress upon everyone your willingness to do any job and to do that job better than anyone else does. Do not waste any time worrying about your ego. The recognition and credit will follow in time. Scoop went on to travel with Governor Clinton on the campaign, and then later with President Clinton managing the entire press corps.

Martha Swiller (then Phipps) was campaign manager David Wilhelm's assistant and my best friend and mentor on the campaign. Martha is younger than I am, but, even in 1991, she had the wisdom and experience to help David manage our campaign. Everyone, no matter his or her status or age, deferred to Martha. On my first day with George, Martha told me to take a three-ring binder and create an assistant's "bible." The bible had to contain everything I might need to know, and it went everywhere with me. Martha showed me how to organize the binder (as I'll show you in chapter 3) so that it contained literally every piece of information I could ever need. Every morning I updated my bible, which helped me familiarize myself with its contents. The point of the bible is simple: You rarely have to answer a question with "I'll get right back to you" (or worse, "I don't know"), because the answer is at your fingertips.

After the campaign, at the age of twenty-seven, Martha became the chief of staff for the Department of Agriculture, one of the largest of the government agencies.

Keep your eyes open for mentors and continually seek them out because you never outgrow the need for a mentor. A mentor is anyone that you admire and someone you aspire to be like. Mentors can inspire you and get you excited about new challenges and possibilities—sometimes ones you didn't even know existed. They can also educate you and answer the most basic questions; for example, in writing this book I'm attempting to be your mentor and help you make the most of your job as an assistant. There are organizations in all major cities which you can locate on the Internet with the goal of helping their members to develop a network of professional contacts and mentors. But you can also find people that you admire and want to emulate at more casual and social events, like dinner parties and book clubs. When you meet someone interesting, be bold and tell her you'd like to stay in touch and get her e-mail address and phone number. Cultivate her friendship. Don't assume that your mentors will just be the obvious people, like your boss. Martha Swiller was my peer in title and status and younger than me, but she taught me a hell of a lot about the fundamentals of my new job and also showed me what it could become.

Who Has Assistants?

In almost all companies and industries, all executives at the level of vice president and above have assistants. Most "directors," and other middle management, take care of themselves, and while they might have employees that report to them, they usually don't have assistants. Different industries have different expectations of their assistants—most dramatically in regard to the amount of personal (as opposed to office) work the assistant does for the boss. I'll talk more about this in chapter 11.

As an assistant your general responsibilities will be to:

- Make your boss more efficient
- Answer the phone and log phone messages
- Manage paper flow into and out of the office (including mail)
- Manage boss's expense accounts and file for reimbursements
- Respond to correspondence
- Set appointments and meetings
- Manage daily and long-term schedules
- Make travel arrangements
- Accept or decline personal appearances (and make recommendations)
- Manage outside consultants
- Gather résumés
- Plan major meetings and conferences
- Manage administrative duties relating to boss's departmental staff
- Maintain files
- Serve as boss's liaison to the public and other departments
- Write memos, bios, letters, etc.
- Edit boss's proposals, reports, etc.
- Collect information and do research
- Assist your boss with whatever projects he is working on
- Manage boss's personal life (depending on your industry and relationship with your boss)

Life After Being an Assistant

A smart manager or executive will groom assistants in his department to move up because talented people trained to the manager's specifications are very valuable, both in the company and as contacts within the industry at another company. If, after being with your company for eight months to a year, you discover that your boss doesn't promote from within the company's ranks of assistants, then learn all you can and leave on good terms with a glowing recommendation. If your goal is to not remain an assistant, then don't take more than two assistant jobs before holding out for what you want; otherwise you might get typecast as an assistant and those will be the only jobs you'll be able to get. If you don't want to continue being an assistant, you must know what you want and be willing to ask for it. So take the time to figure out what job you want next. Look around at the other people in your department who work for your boss, and decide who has the job you want. You're in a perfect position, because knowing what each one of them does is part of your job. It is often much easier to get promoted at your current company because they know your potential, and they've already made an investment in you, rather than convince a new company to take a chance on you and give you a job for which you have no tangible experience. So learn all you can about the company you work for, and if the next job you want is not in your current department, maybe it is in another department within the same company. The more you know about the place you work, the better you'll be at your current job, and the more valuable you'll be to the company as a whole. If you apply for another job within your company for which you have no tangible experience, you have two things going for you that make you a better candidate than another applicant.

You know the company and its product and services, and you've shown that you have an innate ability to learn, and a willingness to work very hard. You'll probably feel as if your next job is a step down when you move from being an assistant to someone of power and influence to being the most junior person in a department. But if your long-term goal is advancement out of the assistant position, you need to gain independence and the responsibility for making decisions. (See chapters 12 and 14 for more about this.)

The qualities needed to be a great assistant are:

- The ability to take control without taking over
- Organization
- Attention to detail
- Diplomacy
- The initiative to solve problems
- Getting satisfaction from being indispensable and in service to someone
- Communication skills
- The ability to stay calm under pressure

If any of these skills comes naturally to you, then you're off to a great start. If a few seem daunting, or if you possess none of these qualities, then keep reading because this book will teach you how to be a kickass assistant.

You've Got the Job, Now What?

Goal: To make your boss as efficient as possible. Do everything you can to make the transition from the former assistant to you smooth, with as little disruption to the boss's world as possible.

It's your first day, and of course you're excited, but you're also a little scared. All right, more than a little. Believe me, I've been there.

I became an assistant in the White House with no grace period for learning anything about the place where I was working. I'd been George Stephanopoulos's assistant for over a year on the Clinton/Gore campaign, but suddenly, on Inaugural Day, 1993, we were starting work at the White House. The phones began ringing immediately, and two enormous mailbags of George's fan mail were delivered that first afternoon. George needed his daily schedule, but we quickly discovered that the computer terminals on the desks were useless because their hard drives had been removed. I needed to pee, but didn't know where the bathrooms were, and I was afraid to walk through the halls of the West Wing. I was sure that one of the uniformed guards would stop me. That first day I sat on the edge of the couch in George's office, which had been every previous White House press secretary's office. When George arrived we stood up and turned on the television and had the surreal experience of watching CNN's live shots of the exterior of the West Wing. They showed the exterior of the window where we were standing watching TV, with a reporter saying something like, "Inside the White House the new administration takes office." I took over the desk outside George's office and looked in the drawers. I found a schedule for President Bush, which was exciting, but I was hoping for something more useful, like Post-it Notes and pencils. I had no idea how to order supplies, nor did I have anyone to ask, as we were all new. Those first days were fraught with tension, not only because of my new job, but also because of the exalted place in which I was working.

About a week after we arrived at the White House, I had to go to the East Wing to run an errand. To get from the West to the East Wing you have to pass through the basement of the residential part of the White House, some rooms of which are on the official public White House tour. About halfway down the main hallway there was a folding screen blocking the width of the hallway. I was sure this was when my fear would be realized; the guard would look at my pass and me and tell me I didn't have clearance to go further. I timidly approached the guard and told him who I was, and my errand, showing him the papers in my hand. He looked at me with incredulity and I prepared myself to be embarrassed and slink back to my desk. The guard explained to me that my pass allowed me to go anywhere in the White House compound (other than the First Family's residence, of course), and that I didn't need to justify my whereabouts to him. I moved around the screen only half believing him, and expecting confrontation from a guard there. But on the other side of the screen was a crowd of tourists dressed in brightly colored leisurewear, in stark contrast to my somber suit and pumps. They stared at me and I at them. I suddenly realized with great clarity that for them, I was part of the tour—a White House staffer—and that the screen was there to keep them out, not to keep me in.

After that I moved around with greater confidence, and slowly began to feel more comfortable in my surroundings. But I can honestly say that as I arrived to work at the White House every morning, I was always amazed to be there. You might not work in an office guarded by armed Secret Service agents and tourists visiting regularly, but when you begin your new job, expect to be overwhelmed and intimidated. You need to compensate for this by being prepared.

Training Period

Ask for a training period with the assistant you are replacing when you accept the job as an assistant. The training period should be no more than a week (five days), but at least two days. Suggest that you arrive at your new workplace an hour after the day has started at the organization. This will allow the soon-to-be-former assistant a chance to get herself settled before you arrive and throw her day into turmoil. Be friendly with the former assistant and find out where she is going, as you might need her help in the future. You should ask about her experience with the company and the boss, and why she is leaving, but be political. It is always better to say less and listen than give away too much information yourself. Pay attention to the way other people, especially your new boss, treat her during your training period: Is she well liked and respected? This will give you an indication as to how much you should take her advice. If she is helpful, ask her about your new boss. How much taking care of does she need? For example: former Clinton campaign manager David Wilhelm is a very smart, but scatterbrained man; when he sneezed, his assistant, Martha, had to hand him a box of tissues. Ask if she helped the boss with errands in her personal life, and if she has any particular boundaries you should be careful not to cross. At the end of your training period, thank her for her help in getting you off on the right foot and ask for her phone number and permission to call her with questions in the future. Don't burn any bridges with thoughtless behavior or comments during this delicate time.

If you don't get a training period, ask for a point person who can help you with questions. The best person would be another assistant who works for a boss of equal stature to your new boss.

Questions to Ask During Your Training Period

The following are questions for which you should get answers as soon as possible. Either copy out these questions or photocopy the following four pages and take them with you. Bring your own pen and notebook, and write down all the answers because you'll be absorbing so much information in the first days and will forget a lot of what you're told. You don't want to ask the same question twice. However, if you don't understand something, definitely ask for another explanation rather than risk doing it wrong.

- **Who's who.** Ask for an overview of who the central characters are in your new boss's life, both personal and professional. One of the easiest ways to do this is to look through the office Rolodex or database together. These are people whose names you should be familiar with, as soon as possible.

- **Ask for an explanation of the phone system.** Find out how the phones work, how the messages are currently recorded, and what is said when the phones are answered. Should you forward the phones to someone else, or to voice mail, when you have to leave your desk? (For example, to run to the bathroom, the copier, or to pick up lunch.)

- **Ask about important dates,** such as birthdays, anniversaries, and regular meetings. Does the soon-to-be-former assistant keep them listed somewhere?

- **Find out about equipment.** Where is it and how does it work? The obvious machines you need to know about are the copier and the fax machines, but perhaps there are others in your new company. For example: color copiers, video conferencing equipment, VCRs, etc. Nothing causes more tension than an impatient boss who wants to watch a video-cassette immediately and you don't know how to operate the VCR. Don't assume that your boss will know how it works—it's very unlikely that he will—and don't assume that you can just put the tape in and push "play" and it'll work. Imagine finding yourself desperately trying to get hold of someone in the audio-visual department and begging them to drop whatever they're working on and run to your office while your boss stands over you fuming. (This scenario actually happened at a company I worked for.)

- **Where do you get supplies?** Are there forms to be filled out, is there an approval you will need, and how long does the process usually take? Is there something you can do if you need an item urgently?

- **What is the boss's schedule in general?** What time does the boss usually arrive at and depart from work? Does she have set daily and weekly meetings?

- **What are the hours of your new job in general?**

- **Where does the boss eat, and typically what time?** Will you be expected to order the boss's lunch, and if so, how do you pay for it? (Does she have a charge account with a restaurant? Do you need to ask her for the money to pay for her lunch up front or can you pay with your own money and be assured of being paid back?) What are some things that the boss likes and does not like to eat and drink?

- **Where is the bathroom,** what are the guidelines for taking breaks?

- **What are the boss's moods?** Is there a best time to get the boss's attention? For example, is the boss a "morning person," or should you try not to talk to the boss until after lunch?

- **Ask for a detailed explanation of the current filing system.**

- **Ask for a discreet overview of the boss's personal life.** For example, is the boss married, does she have kids, where does she live, is there a hobby that plays an important part in the boss's life, etc. Find out as much as you politely can about your boss's spouse and the soon-to-be-former assistant's relationship with that person. It is almost a given that you will be helping your boss out with some areas of her personal life because in the life of a high-powered executive, the lines are often blurred between what is personal and what is professional.

- **How is the mail delivered and when?** Currently, how is the incoming mail dealt with in the office? Do you open everything or are there things your boss prefers to open herself? How do you get it to the boss, and does she want to see everything?

- **Where do you get tech support for the computer?**

- **How do you handle your own and your boss's expense accounts?**

- **Where do you reserve and purchase travel tickets for you and your boss?**

- **Is there a kitchen?** Where do you get coffee? Does the boss drink it, and if so, how?

- **Ask for a company directory.** Take it home and study it to learn who is who, and titles in the company. If there isn't an official company directory, ask for an overview of the company hierarchy. (There will probably be an organizational chart for the executives of the company and possibly for your boss's department).

- **What are your boss's weaknesses?** You need to know so that you can compensate for them. There's a respectful way to ask this, for example: "Does George have any bad habits that I should know about, such as not returning calls promptly, or consistently being late?"

- **What are your options for getting lunch?** When should you get it? Was the former assistant usually able to leave for lunch, or did she eat at her desk?

- **Ask for introductions** to key people that will support you in your new job. For example: the people in the mailroom, the computer tech guys, the travel department, the accounting department in charge of reimbursements, etc.

What to Do and What *Not* to Do

Your first few weeks on the job will be stressful, as there will be a lot to learn. And at the risk of increasing your stress, you need to be aware that you'll be creating a first impression that will stick with you—not just with your immediate boss, but with everyone else you come in contact with. The following are some guidelines of things to do and not to do at work, especially during the first couple of weeks at your new job.

First Week—Do's

- **Admit mistakes and apologize if necessary.** You're going to make mistakes; don't allow your pride to stop you from admitting to them. It's always better to admit to having made a mistake early, and ask for help in fixing it, than to wait until the mistake is discovered (and it will be discovered). When a mistake is discovered you'll look more foolish than if you owned up to it in the first place, and it will be harder to fix the mess you made. (For more on mistakes see chapter 6.)

- **Pay attention to the details.** You'll succeed or fail as an assistant because of your ability to pay attention to details.

- **Answer questions directly, don't ramble.** Give the most succinct and honest answer possible when asked a question.

- **Listen and watch during your training period.** You won't be expected to perform as an assistant, so spend all your energy paying attention to what is happening around you and learning.

- **Take a lot of notes** during your training period and first few weeks on the job because you'll be absorbing a lot of information, and you'll forget things.

- **Be very political.** Watch what you say and how you behave with everyone. It will take you some time to understand all the relationships within the organization where you're working, and in the meanwhile you don't want to form allegiances or insult anyone. Trust no one and do not open up to anyone; offices are full of backstabbers. Avoid cliques, or you could quickly get labeled in a way that you'll later regret.

- **Speak softly.** Someone who talks loudly is annoying and noticeable in a negative way. (There is always someone like this in every office. She invariably sits in a cubicle, so everyone around her is forced to listen to her phone conversations and has trouble concentrating on their own work.) Speaking softly is not only thoughtful, it adds to the impression of calm that you want to present in your office.

- **Plan time alone in the office** as soon as possible, after your training period, to go through everything and take ownership of the space. This will give you a sense of confidence.

- **Dress simply.** You don't want your clothes to be noticed or remembered. Once you have established yourself and earned respect, you'll have more latitude (depending on your industry and company) to express yourself through your dress.

- **Introduce yourself** to everyone you come in contact with, no matter his or her status in the company. First impressions are very important, and to do your job well you will need relationships with everyone from the person who delivers the mail to the CEO. You may find that people aren't particularly friendly toward you, but don't let that intimidate you: Take the initiative and introduce yourself to others. In a perfect world, everyone would be coming up to you to say "hello" and to welcome you but it rarely works out that way.

- **Use your last name** when introducing yourself; it makes you appear serious and grown-up.

- **Pay attention to the way everyone behaves.** Learn the unspoken rules of what is appropriate and what isn't in your new environment. For example, do junior-level employees leave the office for lunch, and if so, for how long are they gone? Do boyfriends and girlfriends stop by the office to visit their partners?

- **Smile a lot.** Smiling makes you appear happy to be there, and approachable. A grump is hard to integrate into the team.

- **Make eye contact** with people you're talking to. Making eye contact shows confidence and honesty.

- Say "**please,**" "thank you," and "you're welcome."

- **Be helpful** to the former assistant as she continues to run the office, while training you.

- **Be prepared to stay late** while you're in training and during the first weeks on your new job. You should never leave the office before your boss.

- **Arrive early** on your first day on your own, after your training period. You'll need some time alone to get comfortable with your surroundings before the business day starts.

- **Stay calm**—take deep breaths if necessary.

- **Look at the newspaper headlines** before you arrive at work. At the most dramatic, it is possible that your boss, company, or industry will be involved in some breaking news that will affect your day. In any regard, it is a good habit to get into, so that you are aware of the world outside your office.

- **Err on the side of caution** when making decisions. Until you know your boss's personality well, and understand her and the company's goals, it's better to make cautious decisions.

First Week—Don'ts

- **Don't assume your new boss likes everything the former assistant does.** It's possible that while your boss was very comfortable with the former assistant, there are things that she'd like done differently. You'll become aware of these things quickly, and you may have an opportunity to ask your new boss if there is anything she'd like you to handle differently than her former assistant did.

- **Don't show your vulnerability,** if you are scared or unhappy. When people at work ask you, "How's it going?" answer, "Great!" with a smile, no matter what the truth is.

- **Don't be star-struck, or jaded.** If you're working in a glamorous environment, it is important to remain professional and not go to either extreme.

- **Don't surf the Internet.** And remember, your e-mail account at work is not your own, it belongs to the company and is for your professional use. Of course, everyone uses their office account to stay in touch with family and friends, just like the telephone, but your e-mails can, and probably will, be read and monitored. You can be fired for inappropriate things you send via e-mail, even to friends outside the company.

- **Don't ask for things like special time off,** special favors, etc. It sets a bad tone early in the relationship. Your new boss will be thinking, "Oh no, is this the way it's always going to be?"

- **Don't chew gum**—ever.

- **Don't make personal phone calls.** There's no hard and fast rule for when it will be appropriate for you to start making personal calls at work, but after the first week you should be able to judge when it is appropriate for you to make a quick personal call. You should always avoid letting your boss hear you on a personal call as it creates a bad impression, and never allow yourself a call of mindless chatter.

- **Don't arrive with luggage.** Particularly in big cities it's common to leave your apartment in the morning and not return until bedtime. There are thousands of women walking the streets carrying a purse, a bag for work, and a gym bag. Eliminate all but one of these for the first few days, otherwise you'll appear disorganized and unprofessional.

- **Don't speak badly of your former boss and/or employer.**

- **Don't be late, or very early** for your training period. Both are equally inconsiderate. It is not always good to arrive early; you can be in the way if the soon-to-be-former assistant isn't ready for your arrival. My advice is to get to the building a little early, and walk around the block until you can arrive at your new office exactly on time or five minutes early.

- **Don't get paranoid if everyone misses the former assistant**— and tells you. People who deal with your new boss will have become reliant upon your predecessor to help them. As much as they miss her as a person, they're reacting to the loss of an important relationship. Don't worry, with your finesse, they'll soon rely equally upon you.

- **Don't distract the soon-to-be-former assistant** as she trains you—remember, she has to keep the office running.

Expect to be confused and overwhelmed during your first days or weeks at your new job. If you are prepared to feel this way it will be easier to handle. If you ask the questions I've suggested here, and any others that occur to you, and if you take my advice and write down the answers, you'll be on your way to being more comfortable in your new workplace. I guarantee that in a month you'll walk into your office building without any of the "new kid" jitters, so as much as you can, enjoy the rush of nervousness and excitement during your early days on the job. And if you can't enjoy the feelings, manage them by concentrating on learning as much as possible about your new world.

chapter 2

How to Give Good Phone

Goal: To make your boss as efficient as possible.
With a little experience and some initiative, you can handle many of the calls that come into your boss's office, and never waste his time with them.

Perhaps the most important area of being a good assistant is managing your boss's phone calls. When you pick up the phone you're creating a first impression for a caller who has possibly never met your boss. Think about that awesome power. As you answer the phone, you can create an impression of the office environment—is everything under control? Try to give every caller the impression that he's your most important call of the day and let him hang up the phone with a very good impression of you, but also with confidence that his message will be relayed accurately to your boss. You have selfish reasons to do this, as the caller might be someone who will speak favorably of you to your boss, or help your career in the future. I called a person I was working with on a project once and as I was trying to leave her a message, her assistant interrupted me to tell me, "I have to hang up now because someone important is on the other line." (My partner on the project also happened to be a personal friend of mine, so you can be sure I repeated the assistant's mistake to her boss.) Being able to control the impression you're creating on the telephone is a skill which will serve you forever. There are several things that will help you to achieve this skill, so consider every phone call an opportunity to practice.

- **Modulate your voice.** Do not speak too loudly into the phone; let your voice be natural, friendly, and pleasant.

- **Listen to the caller,** and do not interrupt. Even if he is asking you the same question you have answered a million times already, and you can see it coming, let him finish before you answer. Do you have any idea how many times I answered the question, "How do you spell Stephanopoulos?"

- **Don't allow stress to show in your voice.** Until it comes as second nature, take a deep breath before you pick up the phone—particularly when the office is busy. Do not allow the caller to feel your nervousness.

- **Use good manners on the phone.** Say "please," "thank you," and "you're welcome." Manners do not make you subservient; rather they show good education.

- **Never eat, drink, or chew gum while you are on the phone.**

- **Do not assume that no one is listening while you are "on hold."**

My friend Charlotte worked at a small P.R. firm and was doing the boring work of calling everyone on a long list to get RSVPs for a party. She had a running joke with a coworker of calling all men "Bob" and all women "Carol"—one of those silly things you do to pass the long hours at work that you can't explain later. She was "on hold" with an assistant who was checking her boss's availability to attend the party. Charlotte got impatient and said: "Come on, Carol, can't you hurry up?" to amuse herself and her listening coworker. The assistant replied icily: "My name's not Carol and I'm doing this as fast as I can." Needless to say, Charlotte was mortified and didn't make a good impression.

Manage the Phone Calls

As always, remember that your goal is to make your boss more efficient. Can you pass on a call to someone else or handle a caller yourself? Certainly you can take care of a call requesting information that you have (a copy of an annual report, a press release, or your boss's birth date). Often people will call your boss who can be referred to someone else for help, particularly someone who works for your boss. You can do this and save your boss the time of returning the call and making the referral. However, if someone that you believe you or someone other than your boss can help really insists that he must speak to your boss only, then definitely put him on the call sheet for your boss. Attempting to protect your boss and save him time is never worth the risk of offending a potentially important caller and making your boss angry. In all areas of being an assistant, judgment comes with experience. It will take you some time to develop a keen sense of which callers genuinely need to get through to your boss, and how quickly.

Learn How to Use the Phone

Don't assume you can figure out how the phone works; take the time to learn. Ask for a thorough lesson and take notes. Make a "cheat sheet" of instructions for yourself; you'll need it when you are busy and nervous, and your boss asks you to place a three-way call. The worst feeling is losing a call as you try to transfer it to your boss. At a minimum, your cheat sheet should remind you of how to put calls on hold, retrieve calls, transfer, and place three-way calls. Type the instructions neatly and put the cheat sheet into your bible (see chapter 3).

Who's Calling?

Find out how your boss likes to know who is calling when he is in the office. There are a few options. Always, always put an incoming call on hold, you don't want the caller to hear your boss telling you he doesn't want to take the call. After you put the caller on hold, you can intercom into your boss's office and tell him who is on the line (this is the most popular method). Or if you are nearby you can stick your head into his office and tell him in person. There are also machines that let you type in the caller's name and it is displayed on a screen on your boss's desk.

The method your office uses will depend a lot on how busy your boss is. If George was in his White House office, he was on the phone. When the phone rang while he was there, I had two options, to take a message or interrupt him on another call. I had to judge if he was on a call that could be interrupted, and if he would want to be interrupted to take the person on hold. It was a constant power game. For example, obviously, no one ever interrupted a call with the president, and anyone could be interrupted for an incoming call from the president. The first lady and one reporter, Ann Devroy of the *Washington Post,* were the only other people who would always take precedence; with everyone else it just depended on who he was talking to and what they were talking about. Making these judgments is a learned skill, but the first step is to pay attention. You must know what your boss is working on, so that you'll be able to judge the urgency of incoming calls. For example, if your boss is dealing with a potentially explosive lawsuit against your company and someone calls from your counsel's office—you'll know to interrupt him for the call. If you're in close proximity to your boss, you can learn who he is talking to from the tone of his voice and listening to a couple of seconds of his dialogue. I was lucky to always be close enough to George to eavesdrop when necessary, and to catch his attention if I wanted to let him know who was on the phone. I usually passed him a note with the name of the caller on hold, and he would indicate with his hands if he wanted to call the person back, or take the call right then. Ask your boss (or if possible, your predecessor) whose calls your boss always takes, and who he will interrupt a call for—the list will probably include family and close friends.

Voice Mail

Use voice mail when you have to leave the office, unless there is someone to whom you can transfer your lines. Don't be dismayed if your boss won't allow you to use voice mail; many bosses worry that important calls won't get through with voice mail and they like the courtesy and luxury of having their phone answered by a human being. They have a legitimate point: you were hired to answer the phone. While answering the phone will chain you to your desk, it's probably the most important part of your job. The best system is to use voice mail only when your boss is out of his office, and you have to leave too (obviously this includes when you go home). Check your messages *as soon as you return* to the office, including first thing in the morning. If you think of something after work hours that you want to remember to do at the office the next day, call your own voice mail and leave yourself a message. You'll find your boss will probably do this too, and you'll get to work and have a message from him telling you three things he needs you to do first thing in the morning. On the rare occasion when you have to leave the office when your boss is still at his desk, have a coworker answer your phone (you can return the favor sometime), or your company may have a formally designated transfer number. Let your boss know that you're leaving your desk, why you're leaving, and that your coworker will be answering his phone in your absence.

Excuses

Ask your boss what excuses he prefers you use for him not taking a call. The most common are that he is on another call or out of the office. If he's not in the office, use discretion in telling a caller where he is. Don't automatically tell the truth, and don't make assumptions regarding who you should tell the truth to. In fact, there are only a few occasions when it's necessary to tell someone exactly where your boss is and what he's doing. *Boundary note: ask your boss who should be told the truth, and in what circumstances.* When we worked in the White House, I lied all the time about George's whereabouts, or was extremely vague. Most often I lied by simply saying I didn't know where he was. Subterfuge was especially important with reporters who would call White House officials and try to piece together what was going on in the West Wing by speaking to hapless assistants and finding out who was in what meeting. Sneaky behavior is by no means limited to the halls of power in Washington, D.C.; people try to weasel information from assistants in the corporate world all the time. And often they don't have to even try because an assistant will offer up information. So be careful. And finally, never tell a caller your boss can't take a call because he's in the bathroom, even if he is. This is more information than anyone needs.

Commonly Requested Information

Post the company's address, contact numbers, and any other commonly requested information near the phone so that you can recite them for callers without thinking (or having to look them up).

Return Calls

Professionalism and good manners require that every call should be returned in twenty-four hours. However, if your boss is notorious for not returning calls promptly, or if you know that he won't be able to return calls because he's traveling or he's in the middle of an overwhelming project, try to give callers a realistic time frame for expecting a return call. However, be careful and don't overpromise. Don't be surprised if your boss returns calls when he knows nobody will be there to take the call (early in the morning, during lunch, after-hours, or on the weekend). This is a pretty common trick to avoid talking to someone.

Building and Keeping a Database

Most likely, your predecessor kept a database of contacts, and you'll be able to continue using her program. However, if there is not a database system in the office, get one immediately. Chances are, you only need something basic, which allows you to input names, addresses (including e-mail) and all phone and fax numbers. All office software packages, such as Microsoft Office and personal digital assistants (like Palm Pilot), have this. You can even create a database using Excel, although this is less helpful when you want to generate specific lists from your database (see chapter 9). You'll also want space for comments in each field. *Never, ever get rid of a single telephone number no matter how trivial it seems.* During the day, write new names and telephone numbers down on your notepad (see chapter 3). At the end of every day (or in a free moment during the day) input the numbers into your database. Make sure to put clues as to who the person is in the comments section because there's a good chance that in a few weeks you'll no longer be able to place the name. If you look up a number of a florist or a restaurant, make a note of the name of the person you spoke to, so that the next time you call, you can ask for them by name and you have created a contact. When you're speaking to someone with whom you think your office will have future contact, or who is important to your boss, ask if you can record his or her contact information for your database (this is a common request). Make sure you ask them if they have the time to stay on the phone with you to give you this information, and make sure that you aren't going to be interrupted while you are talking to them. It's rude to ask them to take the time to stay on the phone with you to give you personal information, and then put them on hold. If necessary, ask for the correct spelling of their name, and then ask for the address where they'd like to receive mail and packages from your boss, their telephone numbers (home, office, car, and mobile), their e-mail address, and their fax number. Don't ask anyone who has their own assistant to give you their contact information; make a note to yourself to call their office and ask their assistant for the information. If you happen to find out personal information (such as a spouse's name) about someone with whom your office has frequent contact, add the information to the comments section under their name. (See chapter 9 for more information on this.) Trust me: Nothing is more powerful than a comprehensive database—if possible, copy this to a disk so you can take it with you when you leave your boss's office.

Creating a Telephone Directory

Your database system will have an option for creating a telephone directory. Make one and put it into a three-ring binder. Put the print date on the first page of the directory, and reprint it periodically as it gets updated with additional new names and numbers. You'll use your computer to look up numbers and addresses most of the time, but having the printout will be necessary for emergencies, if you want to take your database home, or if you're not around and your boss wants to look up a number. However, you should create (and constantly update) a miniature version with only crucial (most called) numbers for your boss to carry in his bag or pocket (illustration number 1). Put another copy near your boss's office telephone, including internal company extensions. George's phone list was taped to his desk under the phone, and I printed his crucial phone numbers onto the back of his daily schedule, which he carried with him all day. Your boss might use an electronic organizer, such as a personal digital assistant or PDA (Palm Pilot, Visor, BlackBerry). If so, then you should input his most called numbers instead of giving them to him on paper.

Below is an example of a miniature telephone directory of most often called numbers, which your boss can carry everywhere with him. It should be one page only and no larger than three inches by six inches—small enough to fit in a jacket's breast pocket or a wallet. If your boss doesn't lose things, go ahead and laminate it—it will last longer that way. If your boss loses everything, don't bother because you will be printing out a new one every day anyway.

James Carville		202-123-4567
Paul Begala		202-123-4567
Stan Greenberg		202-123-4567
	Cell	202-123-4567
Tony Lake		202-123-4567
	Home	202-123-4567
Nancy Hernreich		202-123-4567
	Cell	202-123-4567
	Home	202-123-4567
Wendy Smith		202-123-4567
Ricki Seidman		202-123-4567
Betty Currie		202-123-4567
John Podesta		202-123-4567

Time Zones

Make sure that you understand time zones across the United States. The West Coast is three hours earlier than the East Coast, the Mountain zone is two hours earlier than the East Coast, and the Central zone is one hour earlier than the East Coast. If your company does international business, learn the time zones for the world. You can find them in a telephone directory or on the Internet.

Directory Assistance

Finding telephone numbers by navigating directory assistance worldwide:

- 411—Gets you to your local directory assistance.

- 1-800-555-1212—Gets you to directory assistance for toll-free numbers.

- 1- Area Code - 555-1212—Gets you to directory assistance for the area you are calling. Area codes are listed on pages 42 to 43. Photocopy the illustration and put it into your bible (see chapter 3).

- Internet Directory Assistance—All the major search engines have access to nationwide yellow pages: for example, Yahoo, Lycos, and MSN. Or you can get directly to the directories through yellowpages.com.

- Unfortunately, you have to know what company is your long-distance carrier (MCI, Sprint, Verizon, etc.) to reach international directory assistance. Ask the department in charge of the phone system at your company who your carrier is and write down their name and access number so that when you're looking for a number fast, you already know whom to call. Call your long-distance carrier and ask them to connect you with directory assistance in the appropriate country. If possible, delegate this job, as dealing with telephone operators overseas can be frustrating (if you don't speak the local language). Ask someone on your boss's staff who works with the country in question to get the number for your boss. For example, when I worked for Polo Ralph Lauren I oversaw all the international public relations, and my boss's assistant would always delegate overseas contact to me because I was more familiar with it than she was (and she liked having one less thing to do).

- If the number you need is not going to be available through a directory (such as a celebrity's number), or if you don't know enough information to use a directory service, you'll have to do a little detective work. Think of everyone in your database and start making calls to the people most likely to have the number you need. The bigger your database, the more likely you will be able to locate the number. Remember, never, ever throw away a telephone number. I used to love doing these searches, and would brag that I could get anyone's telephone number in thirty minutes; of course, it helped that I could use George's name. Use your boss's name and the company name to get attention if necessary.

Taking Messages

When you take a message, make sure it is completely accurate. The only way to do this is to 1) pay attention and 2) repeat the important information, especially the caller's name and telephone number, back to the caller. Don't forget to note the time and date of the call on the message sheet. Be aware of your boss's habits and schedule. Do you need to get additional information from the caller, such as other contact numbers and times he'll be available? If you don't know who the caller is, find out. And if you don't know why the caller is calling, find out. But do this diplomatically and naturally. Nothing is more ridiculous (and offensive) than an assistant who says, "And may I tell Mr. Jones what this is regarding?" especially if this is not how you normally speak.

Here's a typical way to ask for the information you need:

Assistant:	"Hello. George Stephanopoulos's office."
Caller:	"Is George there?"
Assistant:	"No, I'm sorry, he's not in the office right now. Would you like to leave a message?"
Caller:	"Yeah, tell him Sam called."
Assistant:	"May I have your last name and telephone number?"
Caller:	"He knows me. But it's Smith and the number is 212-123-4567."
Assistant:	"Thank you, and can I tell George what you're calling about?"
Caller:	"I have some information I think he'll be interested in regarding the conference next week."
Assistant:	"Thank you Mr. Smith, I'll be sure he gets the message. Good-bye."

Boundary note: On your first day you should ask your predecessor or boss for the names of his family and friends who call often. Don't ask these people for information such as why they're calling (if you're very busy, and the caller is friendly, you can nicely ask for their phone number to save you looking it up).

Daily Call Sheets

The most efficient way to generate daily call sheets is through your computer database system. A good system will fill in the phone number when you type in the caller's name; this saves you time and flatters the caller as you don't have to ask for their number. If your boss is comfortable with the computer, he can retrieve his messages from the computer and mark them when he has returned a call. If your boss prefers to receive messages on paper, you can print out his updated call sheet regularly. He should mark the calls he has returned and then you can delete those names from his updated call sheets. If you don't use a computer program to automatically take down messages, you can create your call sheets using the model on page 44. Fill out the call sheets as you take down messages on your computer and save all the dated call sheets on your computer. I don't recommend that you print out blank call sheets and handwrite the messages, because you run a great risk of losing a call sheet and not having a copy. Another method for taking messages is telephone message pad books, which allow you to tear off a slip of paper for every message and leave a carbon master copy. I personally dislike these because the little pieces of paper are easily lost and hard to organize. However, if these are what your boss prefers, try to get him to save the message slips (we used these on the '92 campaign and George would throw them into his out-box after making a call) and put a check on them when the call has been returned. At the end of the day you can review them and make notes on your master copy (the message pad book) of which calls have been returned. *Boundary note: Ask your boss if he wants you to verbally remind him of the calls he neglected to make, or if they should just be put onto the next day's call sheet.* Daily call sheets or message pads are also a good way for you to communicate information to your boss throughout the day; for example, to tell him that his lunch meeting is pushed back thirty minutes or to tell him that his boss has just arrived at your offices. Make sure that you save daily call sheets, whether on your computer or on paper in a file, because at some point your boss will want to find out when someone called.

Also, make sure that you transfer new phone numbers from your daily call sheets to your database (unless you have a computer system that does this for you, which would be nice).

"Urgent"

Use the word "urgent" carefully when relaying messages to your boss. When a caller tells you that his message is urgent, he means that it's urgent to him, not necessarily to your boss. Once you have some experience and develop judgment, you'll quickly know when something really is urgent, but until then ask questions. Ask the caller for a specific timeline on needing a response. When you give the message to your boss, specify that the caller said it was urgent, don't just write "urgent" on the message (the difference is that you aren't telling your boss the message is urgent, the caller is). Notice if your boss returns the call right away or waits; this is how you develop judgment.

Area Codes for Major U.S. Cities

If an area code isn't listed here, you can call directory assistance for an area near the one you want and the operator will tell you the correct area code. They're also listed in the front of telephone directories.

Alabama, Birmingham	205 & 256	San Francisco	415
Alaska	907	Santa Monica	310
Arizona, Phoenix	602	Colorado, Denver	303
California, Burbank	818	Connecticut, New Haven	203
Los Angeles	213	Delaware	302
Oakland	510	Washington, D.C.	202
San Diego	619	Florida, Miami	305 & 786

Tampa	813 & 727	New York, Manhattan	212 & 646
Georgia, Atlanta	404 & 678	Other NYC	
Hawaii	808	Boroughs	718
Idaho	208	Albany	518
Illinois, Chicago	312	North Carolina, Charlotte	704
Indiana, Indianapolis	317	North Dakota	701
Iowa, Des Moines	515	Ohio, Cleveland	216
Kansas, Kansas City	913	Cincinnati	513
Kentucky, Louisville	502	Oklahoma, Tulsa	918
Louisiana, New Orleans	504	Oregon, Portland	503
Maine	207	Pennsylvania, Philadelphia	215 & 610
Maryland, Baltimore	410	Rhode Island	401
Massachusetts, Boston	617	South Carolina, Charleston	843
Michigan, Detroit	313	South Dakota	605
Minnesota, Minneapolis/		Tennessee, Nashville	615
St. Paul	612	Texas, Austin	512
Missouri, Kansas City	816	Dallas	214
Montana	406	Houston	713
Nebraska, Lincoln & Omaha	402	Utah, Salt Lake City	801
Nevada	702	Vermont	802
New Hampshire	603	Virginia, Arlington	703
New Jersey Newark	973	Washington, Seattle	206
Atlantic City	609	West Virginia	304
Trenton	609	Wisconsin, Milwaukee	414
New Mexico	505	Wyoming	307

Below is an example of a daily call sheet. Yours might look different depending upon the computer system that you use, or you can use this illustration as your model and create call sheets on your computer, which you fill in on the computer as you take messages. The status column allows you to mark if the call has been returned, or if a message was left, etc. (FYI: POTUS is White House language for President Of The United States.)

Date	Time	Name	Number	Message	Status
02/05	8:24	James Carville	202-123-4567	Call ASAP	OK
	8:45	Andrea Mitchell	202-123-4567	Wants a comment on POTUS mtg. with Arafat	
	9:04	Jane Brown	202-123-4567	Are you still on for dinner?	L/M
	10:45	Tony Lake	Ext. 7896	Call before 3 P.M. mtg.	
02/06	8:45	Paul Begala	202-123-4567	No message	
	9:03	David Gergen	Ext. 5678	Will be in office for 15 min.	OK
	9:06	Betty Currie	Ext. 3456	Needs help with POTUS schedule	OK

What Does Your Bedroom Closet Look Like? Staying Organized at Work

Goal: To make your boss as efficient as possible by maximizing your own time and efficiency.

You *must* stay organized to be a good assistant. If this comes naturally to you, you're ahead of the game; if not, you must work really hard at being organized. Being organized or not will make or break you as an assistant.

The Essential Notepad

You always need to have a notepad of paper near you. Keep only one notebook or pad of paper at a time to avoid confusion: If you make notes in three different books, you won't know where to find

45

information quickly. Write down everything; don't trust yourself to remember anything. If your boss calls you into her office and tells you to 1) cancel a meeting, 2) invite another participant to a meeting, 3) order her lunch, and 4) bring her the file on international public relations, your notes should look like this:

1)	Cancel 3:30 mtg
2)	Jane Brown @ mkt mtg
3)	Lunch
4)	File - int. PR

Don't assume that you will remember something as basic as ordering her lunch without writing it down; you might be distracted on your way back to your desk, and certainly you will be when you get there and the phone starts ringing. Back at your desk, do the tasks in order of priority and simplicity: While you are ordering her lunch, locate the file on international P.R. Take the file in to her, and then call Jane Brown's office and invite her to the marketing meeting. Cross each of these tasks off the list as you complete them; again, don't assume you'll remember if you actually invited Jane Brown to the meeting, or if you just thought about doing it. Finally, you'll need to make another list of tasks involved in the most complicated task on your list, canceling the 3:30 meeting, and it'll look like this:

> Participants who must be notified:
>
> Mary, Jane, Bob, Sam, John, Fred, Sue, Linda
>
> Cancel use of the conference room
>
> Notify staff member who is putting together the presentation
>
> Cancel food and drink order

Again, cross off each item on the list as you complete it. Remember, while you're completing each task on this list, you're still answering the telephone, interacting with people who come by your boss's office, and responding to additional requests from your boss. Rarely will you be able to complete a task from start to finish without interruption.

I constantly make to-do lists, both in my personal and professional life, to the point that it's a joke among my friends. When something has to get done or be organized, somebody will laugh as they say: "Well, get Heather to make a list." But I can honestly say that I never forget to do anything, and I have a reputation for this. I'm dedicated to the system I'm suggesting you use; I cross things off my lists and update them all the time.

Find a style of notebook you're most comfortable with; some people like spiral bound notebooks and others like legal pads. My advice to you is to use a spiral bound notebook and never tear out the pages, just turn to a clean page. This way you'll never lose any information because you can always search back through the pages to find it. As an assistant, I eventually got to a point of competency at which I could use a legal pad and tear off sheets and throw them away—but this takes a high level of confidence. Periodically throughout the day, update the working page of your notebook by pulling off information and putting it where it belongs, such as telephone numbers into the database and dates onto the schedule. Turn to a clean page in your notebook, put the date in the upper corner, and make a fresh list of what you need to do and remember. Go over the old page carefully; make sure you transfer every piece of necessary information.

Every Morning and Every Evening

Every morning you'll need fifteen minutes of solitude to regroup and organize; make sure you'll have this time before your boss or coworkers arrive. You need to start the day in control. Make sure that you have your to-do list for the day on your notepad, make sure that your boss's schedule is prepared and that you're ready for each event on it, and make sure that both your desk and your boss's desk are in order—do you know where everything is? Every day before you leave the office the last thing you must do is regroup for tomorrow. This will take longer than your morning sessions, and if you have to leave the office before you tie up all these loose ends, make sure you get to the office extra early the following morning.

Steve, who was the assistant to the assistant secretary for Near East and South Asian Affairs at the State Department, told me that he started every day by organizing his boss's desk. He went to the safe where the confidential files were kept, and took out the briefings and files for each region and issue. He laid out the files on the desk in a way that reflected their priority. By organizing his boss's desk this way, he organized his own mind and laid out the day. He was able to move his boss along, telling him what to think about at each moment of the day. Now Steve is an executive at an information company with a huge staff and two assistants of his own. He told me that he wished they prepared him the way he used to prepare his boss. He wishes they looked ahead for him, so that he could apply his thoughts completely to the matter in front of him. One reason it's important to anticipate your boss's needs is because she might not articulate them to you. If you are unsure or not able to anticipate what she needs, don't be afraid to ask her (see chapter 6 on communicating with your boss).

Before the end of every day you must do the following:

- **Clear off your desk.** Put all paper in the appropriate file folders and piles.

- **Clear off your boss's desk,** and clear out her out-box. Look through her in-box and take note of what is still there; make sure there is nothing in the in-box that is timely, but your boss has ignored. *Boundary note: Find out how your boss feels about her desk. Are there things that she prefers you not touch or look through? Find this out before you organize her desk at the end of the day for the first time. She might need time to get comfortable with you and gain confidence in your abilities and discretion before she allows you access to her desk.*

- **Rewrite your daily to-do list.** Turn to a clean page in your notebook and list the things you must do on the following day. Remember to transfer any information you have written there to its appropriate home—telephone numbers into the database and dates onto the schedule.

- **Update your boss's daily call sheet.** As you remove calls she has returned and print out a clean copy, review the list of calls and make sure you are familiar with all of them. Are there any calls you can return for her? Have any of the calls been on the list for too long? Perhaps you should remove the name or return the call yourself and assure the caller he has not been forgotten (for more information, see chapter 2).

- **Print your boss's schedule for the next day.** Make sure it is accurate and that you are prepared for everything on it (for more information, see chapter 7).

Paper

Know what all the paper is on your desk, and make piles of it, but move it off your desk by the end of the day, if possible. For example, organize papers into piles of incoming mail, paper as yet not looked at, invitations and requests pending response, and paper related to specific projects. Put Post-it Notes on top of the piles reminding you, at a glance, of what they are. File paperwork as soon as possible (for more information, see chapter 4) or put papers in their appropriate multicolored file folders to pass between you and your boss (for more information, also see chapter 4).

Multitask

"Multitask" is one of those modern buzzwords that can be overused, however it does represent an important skill for the successful assistant. You must learn to accomplish several things at one time, without losing track of any of them. The best way to do this is to make notes of what you are doing to remind yourself as you switch gears from one thing to the next. For example, you'll almost certainly never be able to do anything during the workday without also answering the telephone, and complying with the requests of your boss. Remember, while the individual tasks you're doing, such as answering the telephone and filing paperwork, may not be terribly challenging by themselves, the ability to do everything at one time (and do it all fast and well) is the challenge.

Block Your Time

Look at your tasks as individual projects and block out time to get each one done all at once during your day. This will keep you organized and efficient. If you start several daily routine tasks but don't finish any of them before starting another, you'll find yourself confused and your desk a mess. For example, know what time the mail is delivered and plan to open and sort it all at one time.

Plan to be at your desk while your boss is in the office, and plan to run errands while she's out. It will frustrate her not to have you at your desk when she needs you, and seeing your empty chair (no matter what the reason) creates a bad impression. Look at your boss's schedule and your own to-do list in the morning and try to coordinate them. Cluster the errands you have to do away from your desk for a block of time when she's out of the office. For example, save all your photocopying to be done at one time or plan a trip to the mailroom based on a time when she's gone, but that will still get your deliveries out on time.

Lists

Make lists constantly and always make them in your notebook. Obviously, the most important one will be your to-do list, but make lists of anything you need to remember. You'll want to keep a running list of questions for your boss, so that you're prepared to take advantage of any opportunity to talk to her. If you run a very busy office, you might need to manage several to-do lists concurrently; for example, a list of personal things to do for your boss (pick up her dry cleaning, get her car detailed, buy a present for her niece, etc.), a list of things to do related to a conference you're organizing (book hotel, interview caterers, schedule speakers), and a to-do list related to the running of the office (file boss's reimbursement forms, send flowers to Joe, confirm weekly marketing meeting). Organizing your tasks in this way will make them seem more manageable and gives you an immediate way to prioritize them.

Watch the Clock

Always be aware of what time it is and deadlines throughout the day. You should be conscious of your boss's schedule so that you can appropriately time when to make her aware of something, or, if need be, to move her along in her duties.

Your Bible

One of the best tools for staying organized is a three-ring binder, which contains all the information you need at your fingertips. On the Clinton for President campaign, the assistant to the campaign manager and I called them our bibles. I worked with another guy once who called it his "Book of Life." Whatever you call it, you'll need one. You'll come up with your own personalized version, which will have what you need to be highly organized, but the following should definitely be included, separated by dividers.

- **Company telephone directory**—this is the official one printed by your company
- **Database telephone directory**—this is the collection of names and numbers from your boss's office
- **List of your boss's immediate staff** with their titles and personal information (including home numbers)
- **List of your boss's personal information,** including addresses, date of birth, social security number, driver's license number, credit card numbers, and passport number. *Boundary note: Make sure your boss wants you to have*

this information, and if you have it, you must guard it carefully.

- **Emergency contact numbers,** including your boss's doctors and lawyers
- **List of your boss's family and friends** and their contact numbers
- **List of most often called business associates,** including coworkers at your company and their home numbers
- **A printout of your boss's daily schedule**
- **A printout of your boss's long-term schedule**
- **A list of the projects your boss is working on,** and any pertinent information

Any of the above lists that do not change daily should be laminated or put inside clear plastic pages to protect them, as they'll quickly become worn. Remember, this book includes a lot of personal information about your boss and others—keep it private.

Staying organized will allow you to do your job well because being organized will make you efficient. Once being organized is second nature to you, you'll be able to take on new and more challenging projects because the mundane clerical work of your job will be under control. And training yourself to be organized will benefit you in every job you will ever have.

Don't Be a
Paper Pusher

Goal: To make your boss as efficient as possible.
Do not allow your boss to be slowed down
by mountains of paper.

Stay on Top of the Paper Flow

To be a great assistant, you have to be able to get
your hands on anything within minutes, and this
includes all the paper that has moved through your
office—ever. The paper that comes into an office
can be overwhelming, and while you don't want
your boss to be slowed down by paper, *you* don't
want to be demoralized yourself by the amount of
paper you have to manage. The key is to stay organized and stay on top of it—don't ignore incoming
paper and allow it to pile up. If you do this, you'll
find that you have overlooked and lost important
documents, and the idea of organizing the piles of

paper will seem completely depressing and impossible. You must have a system for managing incoming paper, and at a certain point, when it is no longer needed every day, your paper will need to be filed within close proximity to you. And then, at a later date, when you'll never or rarely need them, your files can be purged and put into storage.

Incoming Paper

The paper coming into the office will be:

- Memos and reports sent via interoffice mail
- Faxes
- Magazines and newspapers
- Paper your boss brings into the office from trips and meetings. (How to handle e-mail and traditional mail correspondence is covered in chapter 5.)

How to Handle All the Incoming Paper:

- **Route it directly to your boss's in-box:** Both you and your boss should have in-boxes and out-boxes on your desks. The in-box on your desk is for everything that comes to you, to your boss, and to the office in general so put it in an obvious place where people can find it if you are not at your desk. Nothing should go directly into your boss's in-box without your knowledge. You need to control what is in her in-box because:

  1) You are managing her time, and paper takes time. Often something can be dealt with by you, or someone else.
  2) If something goes into her in-box without your

knowledge, you can't track it. It could get lost, or the person who sent it could ask what action your boss took and you'll have no idea.

3) You'll lose the opportunity to educate yourself by being aware of what your boss is working on.

People will try to bypass you and your system. They'll put things directly into your boss's hands, and into her in-box if you aren't at your desk. Ask people (especially your boss's staff) not to do this. Explain that it's in their best interest to go through you because later, when they want to know the status of their request/report/memo, you won't be able to help them if you aren't aware of it. Make sure that people want to work with you and that you aren't an obstacle they feel they have to work around; don't be rude or controlling, and don't lose things they put into your hands. These are all common complaints lodged against executive assistants by the other people who work for the executive. Use multicolored file folders, labeled to organize the paper going to your boss.

Make a file for each of the following categories of paper:

1) For Your Signature
2) Mail
3) Memos and Reports
4) Reading
5) Call Sheets

And any others that are appropriate for your industry.

- **Maintain consistency in the colors** of each of these files so that your boss will eventually recognize the contents by the file color rather than by reading the label. You also need to have total control over your boss's out-box. Hopefully, she'll put all paper exiting her office in it and you'll clean it out several times a day. Deal with what's in her out-box immediately; for this system to work, your boss needs to know that the paper in her out-box won't languish there for several days. Showing initiative is one of the qualities that separates an okay assistant from a great assistant, and managing your boss's in-box gives you another opportunity to do this. If every day you put unsolicited proposals from vendors into your boss's in-box, and she consistently writes "Send to Maria" on them and puts them into her out-box, you can take the initiative to eliminate your boss from the cycle and send the vendors' proposals directly to Maria.

- **Deal with it yourself.** This includes correspondence for which you can generate a response without your boss's input (see chapter 5).

- **File it:** see below

- **Throw it in the garbage.** Be very, very careful of this, especially at the beginning of your career as your boss's assistant. In fact, I suggest that you have a garbage pile in the corner of your office/cubicle or under your desk where you put paper you believe to be garbage (including newspapers and magazines). After paper has sat in the pile for a week or more, you can safely put it in the garbage for permanent removal. This doesn't include most reports and memos generated internally because you can get copies for your boss should she request them, so they can be thrown out as soon as she is done with them.

Help Your Boss with Information Overload

Depending upon your boss's nature and workload, she might appreciate having a brief summary attached to memos and reports. This is especially true if the subject of the memo isn't very apparent on the front page in bold. It's easy to simply attach Post-it Notes to the fronts of memos with a quick explanation. If you put a report into your boss's in-box, which she didn't request, and which is long, she might appreciate a summary of several sentences. However, a word of caution: Judge your own time constraints; don't allow a report addressed to your boss to sit in your pending pile of paper for several days as you try to find the time to do a summary. If you can't do a summary quickly, it would be much better that you put it directly into your boss's in-box. At the top of memos you'll see the name of the sender and recipient and then a list of names under "cc," which stands for carbon copy, and is the entire group who the memo has been sent to. Memos sent directly to your boss, as opposed to cc'd to her, should be afforded greater attention. (Pay attention to the cc list, and don't send it back to people who have already received a copy of it.)

George always read newspapers and magazines quickly and voraciously; he certainly didn't need my help in this. However, I have had a couple of bosses since who wanted my help in reviewing the mountains of newspapers and magazines that come into an office. If your boss doesn't have the time to read everything immediately, it is particularly important that you scan the papers and magazines (including trade publications) for articles that pertain to your boss and her work. Highlight these and put them in her in-box (or if it is very timely and important, in front of her), so that she is informed and not caught off guard by someone else who has already seen the article.

Paper Your Boss Generates

Your boss's handwritten notes on scrap paper, such as the back of her daily schedule, can be very important. George was in the habit of never throwing anything with his notes on it away; instead he threw it into his out-box. He knew I'd scan it for information and then file it. I'm sure he did this because he was acutely aware of the historical context in which we worked, and in fact, years later he had voluminous papers to search through when writing his book. However, this habit can be really helpful even if your boss isn't planning to write a memoir. For example, at the end of the day George would throw his daily schedule into his out-box. He had carried it around all day and it would have notes on it, such as needing to make a call, write a note to someone, or set up a lunch. George would empty his pockets when he got back to the office, and I would empty his travel bag when he got back from a trip; I would find business cards (all the information went into our database), scraps of paper (one with the name of someone to whom he had promised to send a "signed" photo of Socks the cat), and other fun stuff. *Boundary note: Ask your boss if you may sort through her papers and briefcase when she returns from a business trip. Make it clear why you want to do it. She may not initially be comfortable with you doing this and may have to reach a higher level of confidence in your discretion before she agrees.*

Financial Paper

You'll need to keep track of all of your boss's financial paperwork. This includes bank account and expense account statements that come in the mail, and receipts that she brings back from meetings, meals, and trips. (Your tracking of these receipts, and filing for their reimbursement, is another motivation for your boss to empty her pockets into her out-box and to allow you to go through her briefcase.)

Educate Yourself

Read all the reports and memos that come into the office. If this is unrealistic, at least scan everything to get a general understanding of it. It's worth taking the time after hours to do this because you'll learn a lot both about the style of writing memos and reports, and also the issues themselves. After all, access to power and information is why being an assistant is a good education. So take the time to educate yourself. And finally, keeping abreast of the issues your boss is working on will only make you a better assistant. Imagine the great impression you would make if your boss asked your opinion about something and you actually had recently read something on it and could make an informed response!

Filing

Remember, you have to be able to get your hands on anything within minutes, and this includes all the paper that has moved through your office—ever. To do this effectively, you not only need a good system to get the paper coming into the office to your boss and back out of the office, you also have to have a system for filing it for future use.

If you have any doubts as to the importance of filing papers for easy and quick retrieval, pay attention to this story. In the summer of 1996, the press reported that the White House had requested over three hundred FBI background files, including some on prominent Republicans. The White House responded

that the inclusion of Republicans on the list was a simple clerical error; they had all at one time worked in the White House.
It's routine for the White House to request copies of background files on its current staff, but it seemed suspicious for
them to be requesting FBI files on big-name Republicans, especially during President Clinton's reelection campaign. The man
who requested the files from the FBI was Craig Livingston, the
head of White House Security. Of course, Republicans were
furious and called for investigations and apologies, and the
press began to investigate Craig Livingston's background.
Livingston worked on the Clinton campaign in '92 in some for-
gettable capacity, and managed to get a job as a low-level func-
tionary in the White House Personnel Office after we won. In
investigating Livingston's request of FBI background checks,
the press rightly began asking questions as to how and why
Livingston had been promoted to be the head of White House
Security. (There was the implication that he had played a role
in the disappearance of alleged missing files after Vince Foster's
suicide and the promotion was a payoff for his work).
Livingston claimed that George had helped him get his promotion, and for a day the press was all over George hoping for a
story on his involvement in this mess. I watched this scandal
unfold from Austin, Texas, where I was working on Clinton's
reelection campaign. That evening on the network news a
White House correspondent held up evidence that George had
released proving his innocence. The evidence was a memo
Livingston wrote to George requesting his help in getting the
job as head of White House Security. On the memo was a Post-
it Note, which read in my handwriting: "G.—Do you want to
do anything about this? H." There, on national television, was
George's written response to me, "No." I had filed the memo
over a year earlier and it had been retrieved.

* * *

Maintaining a paper trail by keeping comprehensive files is important for staying organized, but can also be critical for job survival. Your boss will question how you handled certain things and his boss in turn will question how he handled something. The best response to being questioned is to be able to show paper to the boss. For example: Your boss's mother is on the board of directors of a children's charity and she's just called him and asked what happened to her request for help with their fundraiser. When your boss calls you into his office he's on the offensive because he's worried he may have let his mother down. If you keep good files you'll be able to pull the original letter seeking a donation, a printout of your e-mail to the public relations department requesting that a check be sent, and the response that it will be taken care of. Your boss will calm down and be able to call his mother and tell her in complete confidence that everything is taken care of. (You already called his mother and told her the check would be coming after you talked to the P.R. department, but she needed to hear it from her son.) Now imagine the same scenario but with your boss in the hot seat being questioned by his boss. He will come immediately to you for the quick proof that he handled a situation and you will turn to your files and hand him the paperwork he needs.

Files

You should have three sets of files:

- **The Main Office Files**—this includes files for your clients, consultants, ongoing projects, correspondence, general company information, press releases, minutes from meetings, and résumés of potential employees.

- **Your Boss's Personal Files**—this includes files for her financial data, real estate, medical data, private projects, and her résumé. *Boundary note: Make sure that you keep files on your boss's personal life with her permission and keep this file cabinet locked if possible.*

- **Your Personal Files**—this includes files of forms (shipping, health insurance, reimbursements, etc.), fax cover sheets, vacation ideas, lists of restaurants, and your résumé.

Each file should be labeled with an obvious name, and filed alphabetically. If a file gets full, do not overstuff it; start a new file labeled with the same name and "continued," and put it immediately behind the original file. Within a file folder, file documents chronologically.

Things to File

Keep a "to-file" pile of paper and make the time to file at least once a month. If your office has slow days (for example when your boss is traveling or at an all-day meeting), take the opportunity to file. However, if you work in an office which is constantly busy, you will have to plan to come in on a weekend to get the filing done. Unfortunately, filing isn't something that can be done successfully during a busy day, while you're doing other things like answering the phone and ordering lunch. If you don't pay close attention to what you are doing, you'll file something incorrectly, and it will be lost forever. You'll be more successful and confident in your work if you come into the office in jeans on a Saturday, turn on the radio, and take your time spreading out all the paper and making order of it.

Know Your Files

While filing is a boring and dull task, it's very helpful to be familiar with everything that is in your office files, and the only way to be familiar is to have done the filing yourself. If you work in a very busy office, and the filing is so overwhelming that it justifies hiring a temp once a month, or if you have interns working for you, make sure that you work with them and know what is filed and where. If you have someone helping you with the filing, I suggest that you go through each document and write at the top what it should be filed under, then hand it off to have it actually filed in a labeled file folder. This way you will be familiar with documents and their file names.

Master List

Another helpful tip is to create a master list of all your files, and if necessary a description of what is in each file. Just type the list into your computer.

Purge the Files

Every six months (or more frequently depending on your file space), you'll need to purge your files and put them into storage. A great time to do this is while your boss is on vacation because she probably won't be calling in several times a day, and things will slow down in the office. Again, if this isn't an option, you'll need to go in to the office on a weekend. Your company should have a storage facility that can supply you with file boxes; if not, you can order them from any office supply store. Work with your office manager or an admin person who can probably help you with this. Before you embark on this project, check with your boss to see if she has opinions as to what files can go into storage and what she wants to remain more accessible. (Most bosses won't care to get involved, but they will care if they want something and you can't produce it quickly). Also, check with your company's legal department and make sure you are clear on what files must be saved, and what (if any) don't need to be saved. And pay attention to the security of confidential files; don't send any files that were kept in a locked filing cabinet to a warehouse in a cardboard box.

Do It Right

Don't get lazy and just shove papers into the filing cabinet hoping for the best. Take the time to do this right.

What the Last Assistant Left Behind

If you inherit a mess of disorganized files from your predecessor, then you'll have to sort through it all. However, start small; start new files with the above system and treat the original, disorganized files as archives. After you've been in your job for a month or two, and you're feeling comfortable about other areas of the job, schedule a few weekends to deal with the old files. Take them out a few at a time and look through the documents carefully. Integrate the files that are well organized into your filing system, start an archive box of files to go to storage, and refile important documents into your files. Create a pile of documents that you believe to be garbage, and ask your boss to go through it. Let her know that you are working on the big project of updating the filing system. Obviously you'll have to thoughtfully pick the time to ask her to help you, otherwise she'll think it is a waste of her time. She might think this anyway, and leave you to sort it out on your own. If this is the case, just box everything up that you aren't sure about, and send it to storage.

Filing E-mail

There is a more detailed discussion of e-mail in the next chapter, but don't forget that a great deal of important information is passed through e-mail, and while it may never get printed out, it should be filed for later retrieval. E-mail is often like a recorded telephone conversation, and while you don't have the opportunity to record and file your phone conversations for later retrieval, you can do this with e-mail. File your e-mail electronically in your e-mail system, using folders. Unlike your paper files, you can pick a filing system that is very personal because no one other than you will have access to it. You can file your e-mails by subject, by the name of the sender, or chronologically. The goal is simply that you can retrieve something quickly and easily, so use a system that makes sense to you. Don't forget to file e-mails you have sent as well as those you have received. It can also be useful to keep your "trash" folder accessible for several weeks (just like your paper trash) before you delete it permanently. And just like your paper files, your e-mail files should be purged periodically. Go through them every month or so, and delete anything you feel is no longer useful.

chapter 5

Put It in Writing: Electronic and Paper Correspondence

Goal: To let your boss focus on his job, and allow his mind to be uncluttered by the clerical work of correspondence.

This chapter deals with paper correspondence via the U.S. Post Office, FedEx, UPS and couriers, and electronic mail. As always, your goal is to maximize your boss's time, and to do everything for him that you can, so unless it is absolutely necessary, don't give him mail that he will have to 1) read, 2) make a decision on, and/or 3) take action on, without sorting it first (see page 70). Consider that by handling your boss's correspondence, you're doing his personal public relations. The P.R. department of your company exists to benefit the company, not your boss (unless your boss is the company—like Ralph Lauren at Polo Ralph Lauren, or the president at the White House), so you need to take responsibility for your boss's P.R.

On our first day in the White House two enormous U.S. postal bags were delivered to my desk full of George's fan mail that had been arriving at the White House since Clinton was elected two and a half months earlier. George had received a lot of mail on the campaign, and dealing with it was a real headache, but his campaign mail was nothing compared to what he received at the White House. Hundreds of new letters arrived every day and I was thrilled to find a department listed in the White House directory called the White House Correspondence Office. With relief I called them to let them know I needed some help; however, I was quickly informed that they only handle mail addressed to the president or members of the First Family. Socks the cat got his mail answered by the White House Correspondence Office, but not George Stephanopoulos.

Although I have no formal research to back this up, I'm confident in saying that no staff member of any White House administration before or since has had the kind of fan following that George did. For many people, I'm sure George seemed more approachable and accessible than the president. George's mail was simply an extension of the president's mail, and many people wrote to him because they felt a connection with him after seeing him on the evening news almost nightly. I wanted to petition the Chief of Staff's office to make an exception and allow George's mail to be answered by the White House Correspondence Office, but George wouldn't let me. He didn't want to ask for any special favors.

I found the best solution I could, given my resources (zero). I recruited a team of interns, who frankly were cheated out of the great experience they expected to get as White House interns and were used by me as free labor. I begged for extra office space and was given a tiny space in the attic (literally) of the Old Executive Office Building, the annex to the White House. Every day I sorted about a hundred pieces of mail that came in without opening them, judging them merely by the envelopes. Only about 5 percent stayed with me in our West Wing office, the rest I sent over to the OEOB. I got pretty good at pulling out the timely and important mail, and doing this taught me some lessons about outgoing mail that are important when you want your piece of mail to get the right kind of attention—such as when you are sending out your unsolicited résumé:

- Never send anything simply by mail to an office
- Follow up your mailed correspondence with a fax or e-mail
- Telephone to confirm receipt
- Make the envelope and letter appear as professional as possible
- Do not handwrite any part of the address
- If you make a mistake, start again with a new envelope
- Use professionally printed envelopes with your return address (if possible)

I trained our interns to sort through the incoming mail which I sent over to the OEOB, by opening and categorizing it. They decided upon the appropriate response letter from a set of form letters which I had written, and generated the letters and envelopes. I reviewed them and signed George's name. (This was my opportunity to pull out any letters that required George's real signature or a nonform letter response.) We were processing hundreds of letters a day with no real professional

resources and I felt very alone in this mission. I'm not sure
George even realized how much mail he got. Maybe I was
naïve, but I was convinced that it would be damaging for both
George and the administration for these letters to be ignored
and so I took the initiative to solve the problem as best I could.
I learned that I had to stay organized and disciplined to manage the volumes of mail that came in every day, but also that I
had to be determined that the project was worth all the effort it
required. If you really believe in a project sometimes you have
to work on it against the odds.

Incoming Paper Mail

There are two categories of both paper and electronic mail
about which you must worry. Mail that is coming in, and that
which you are sending out.

1) **Open everything.** *Boundary note: Ask your boss if there is
   any mail you should never open; for example, his bills or anything marked "personal."*

2) **Staple envelopes to letters and all enclosures.** This is
   important—you don't want to separate the letter from any
   of the materials sent with it, and you don't want to lose the
   envelope. An envelope contains information which can be
   important, such as the return address and the postmark. (A
   postmark gives you the date and location from which the
   mail was sent.)

3) **Write the current date on the incoming letter** or get a
   "received" stamp with the date on it; this will help you
   track the letter and its response. If you have anyone working with you, such as another assistant or an intern, have

him put his initials next to the date so that you'll know who opened the letter.

4) **Sort the mail** into the following categories:

Category 1. Mail that your boss must look at before you take any action, or for which no action will be needed. This will include personal mail to your boss, speculative mail—for example, pitch letters trying to get business with your company—and possibly complaint letters, which can go to your customer service department after your boss has seen them. A lot of this will be junk, but you'll need experience to know what, if anything, will be interesting to your boss. Some of this speculative mail you might want to file for your future use, such as a brochure on a conference center, in case you are called upon to organize a meeting. Put explanations on Post-it Notes on the pieces you give to your boss, for example: "Information from a company which builds web pages." Put all this into the Mail file folder (one of your colored file folders—see chapter 4).

Category 2. Mail for which you can immediately generate a response for your boss's signature, such as a thank you or request for information. Generate the appropriate letter (standard form letters should be saved on your computer) and the return envelope, then paper clip these to the original incoming letter, enclosures, and envelope. Put these letters into the For Your Signature file (one of the colored file folders). Make sure that you use a paper clip and not a staple to attach the outgoing letter to the incoming letter (staples are too difficult to remove and leave ugly holes). Make sure that you generate the return envelope at the same time that you write the letter; it will save time later. Getting your boss to sign the outgoing letters in a timely fashion is your responsibility—don't let the letters linger on his desk for too long. It's easy for him to sign routine letters while talking on the phone.

Proofread the form letters that you prepare very carefully before you give them to your boss for his signature. Use the Spell Check and Grammar Check tools on your computer. Make absolutely sure that you spell the recipient's name correctly and that you get their gender correct (Ms. or Mr.?). If you are in any doubt, try to call and check. Common mistakes in generating form letters occur because you haven't made all the necessary changes from the last letter you wrote using the form letter. If you find that you make a lot of errors, get a coworker (another assistant) to proof your letters as well. Nothing wastes time, and creates a bad impression, like having your boss catch your typos.

Category 3. Invitations. Printed invitations can go into the Mail file folder immediately. The easiest way to handle them is for your boss to look through them and simply write "yes" or "no" on each one. You can then call and RSVP for him, throw out the declines, and mark the "accepts" on the calendar. Save the invitations that you say "yes" to (see chapter 7) because your boss might want to see them before the event, as they contain a lot of information (such as the dress code).

Category 4. Mail that needs response from your boss before generating the letter, such as a request to speak or for a donation. These letters should go into your Pending file folder. Create a memo for your boss like the one below listing questions; once you get answers from him, you can generate outgoing letters for his signature, as above. It's possible that you'll have to contact the sender of the letter for more information before you can get an answer to her inquiry. For example, if an organization sends a request for your boss to speak to them, you might need information about the event or the organization which wasn't included in the letter.

Your memo to your boss should look something like this:

January 8, 2002
TO: George
FR: Heather
RE: Requests

- Request to be the keynote speaker at the MADD annual conference on February 10, 2002 in Orlando. They expect an audience of 500 including members of the press. Will pay all expenses, but no speaker's fee. You do not have any scheduling conflicts.

  Accept_____ Decline_____

- Request for a donation to the HVA (Housatonic Valley Association) annual fundraising auction. They are requesting a company product of a value of at least $40. Last year we contributed clothing from Polo Jeans valued at $500.

  Make Donation_____ Decline_____

- Request for a tour of our offices by a local Girl Scout troop.

Category 5. Anything financial, such as bank statements, bills, credit card statements (either personal or corporate), etc., put into the Financial file folder to be managed by either you or your boss. *Boundary note: Does your boss want you to manage his personal bills and/or his corporate expense accounts?*

Category 6. Junk Mail. Until you are confident in your job, err on the side of caution and don't throw anything away unless you are sure it's truly junk mail.

Outgoing Paper Mail

The following are the types of correspondence you will be sending out from your office:

1) **The letters you have generated in response to incoming mail.**

2) **The letters your boss wants to send out.** Pay attention to the letters you're receiving—which ones are well written and why. Copy their style when you're writing similar letters. Look at letters that have been sent out from your office in the past and use the same format. However, if this isn't possible, your computer program will have a guide for formatting letters. (In Microsoft Word it is called Letter Wizard and is located in Tools.) The best letters I've ever read always tell me what the writer wants within the first three sentences. When you're writing a letter, get to the point quickly, and don't make the busy recipient read two paragraphs before he knows who you are and what you want.

3) **The final category of outgoing mail is handwritten notes.** You should have a stash of note cards of the company sta-

tionery to use for handwritten notes. Depending on your boss, you may need to suggest when he should send out handwritten notes, as opposed to typed letters. Here are some guidelines for when handwritten notes should be sent: in response to a gift, congratulations, condolences, and thank you for something special or personal—such as a lunch or dinner. A handwritten note should be sent to anyone with whom your boss wants to ingratiate himself. As with everything in this book, what is true for your boss is true for you: Take the time to write handwritten notes to people whenever appropriate. Use all the same guidelines that you use for your boss. Pay attention to the newspapers, trade papers, and gossip and let your boss know if there is someone who he should be sending a note to (for example: someone who he used to work with who has moved to another company). Paper clip a blank note card to an addressed envelope and put a Post-it Note on the card telling your boss to whom he should write and why. (For example: "Condolence note to Sally in Accounting who always puts a 'RUSH!' on your reimbursement checks. Her father died over the weekend.") Put all the note cards in the For Your Signature file folder (another colored file folder).

Creating a Paper Trail

When your boss returns the For Your Signature file folder, photocopy every letter (including the handwritten ones) and staple the photocopy to the original incoming letter, enclosures, and envelope. These are ready to file (see chapter 4 for a discussion on why creating a paper trail and maintaining files is so important). The signed letters are ready to put into their envelopes and mail out.

The Mailroom

Your company will have a mailroom and you must be on good terms with the people who work there. During your first few days at your new job, go meet them in person. Learn their names and treat them with respect; the people working in the mailroom can make you look good or bad because they are crucial support staff for your office. Ask for their rules for out-going mail—these may include forms or labels to be filled out for anything going overnight or express delivery. Ask them about the deadlines by which you must get outgoing mail to them for it to reach its destination. You can't cheat on these times, and neither can the mailroom. Certainly, they'll leave themselves some wiggle room in these deadlines, but don't take advantage of this unless it's an absolute emergency. If your inefficiency causes you to have to beg favors, or worse, scream and yell to get your boss's mail to its destination on time, you're doing something very wrong. If you miss a deadline for a critical shipment, you will have to do the work yourself and your options will be: find and call a courier (your mailroom may have on-site messengers or be able to recommend a service), go to a shipping service office (FedEx, UPS, U.S. Post Office, etc.), or deliver the package yourself if it is within driving distance.

Form Letters

The next few pages contain examples of standard form letters for most needs. I suggest you type them into your computer, make appropriate changes, and save them on your hard drive. This way you can generate response letters on your company's letterhead fast. Don't forget to generate the response envelope at the same time. Always include your boss's title after his name

above the signature line, unless he has personal company sta-
tionery that lists his title on the letterhead.

January 26, 2002
Mary Brown
Mothers Against Drunk Driving
1234 Main Street
City, State, Zip

Dear Mrs. Brown,

Thank you for the invitation to speak at your annual
convention.

I must decline due to scheduling conflicts. However, I
applaud your work, and please keep me in mind as a
speaker at future events.

Sincerely,

George Stephanopoulos, Senior Advisor to the
President for Policy and Communications

GS/hb

January 26, 2002
Mary Brown
Mothers Against Drunk Driving
1234 Main Street
City, State, Zip

Dear Mrs. Brown,

Thank you for the invitation to speak at your annual convention.

I am flattered and am pleased to be able to accept. My assistant, Heather Beckel, will contact you to make arrangements and confirm the details. However, please feel free to contact her should you have any questions (telephone: 202-456-1234).

Sincerely,

George Stephanopoulos, Senior Advisor to the President for Policy and Communications

GS/hb

January 26, 2002
Mary Brown
PS 4 – Fourth Grade Class
1234 Main Street
City, State, Zip

Dear Mary,

Thank you for your interest in the White House and my background.

As you requested, I am sending you my biography and some information on the history of the White House. Good luck with your school project.

Sincerely,

George Stephanopoulos, Senior Advisor to the President for Policy and Communications

GS/hb

January 26, 2002
Mary Brown
1234 Main Street
City, State, Zip

Dear Mrs. Brown,

Thank you for your letter. The opinions of our customers are very important to us here at Sam Smith Industries.

I have passed your letter to our customer service department and have asked them to look into your complaint and get back to you as quickly as possible. Should you wish to contact them, they can be reached at 216-345-6789.

Sincerely,

Sam Smith, President and CEO

SS/hb

January 26, 2002
Mary Brown
Mothers Against Drunk Driving
1234 Main Street
City, State, Zip

Dear Mrs. Brown,

Thank you for giving me a chance to participate in your silent auction.

I am enclosing my signed "doodle art" as a donation to your event. Best wishes for a successful fund-raiser.

Sincerely,

George Stephanopoulos, Senior Advisor to the President for Policy and Communications

GS/hb

Incoming E-mail

The way you manage e-mail will depend almost entirely upon your boss, and how comfortable he is with it. Most bosses nowadays are very comfortable with e-mail and find it an efficient way to work. However, at the time I worked for George, he only checked his e-mail infrequently, and didn't have the patience or time to type responses. So I printed things I knew he would want to see and put them into his in-box. He would write his response in his shorthand on paper and put it into his out-box. Then I'd get the response to the appropriate person, either by e-mail or verbally. E-mail can screw up your system of controlling documents going to your boss, because people will e-mail them directly to him and never put them on paper. If you never see the e-mails being sent to your boss, you won't be able to edit them and stop people from wasting his time and you won't know what's going on. Hopefully, two things will happen in your office: First, your boss will let you have access to his e-mail account and, in fact, want you to edit what gets to him in the same way you edit his in-box. In some companies it may be possible for your boss to have a "public" e-mail address that comes to you, as well as a confidential address that you can use to forward important mail to him and that he can use to communicate with friends and family privately. Second, people will "cc" you on documents they send to your boss. Work with your boss's staff and other people sending him regular e-mail correspondence and ask them to cc you on their e-mails to him. Explain that having access to these documents will help you to manage the office better because you'll be able to track them and eventually file them. If necessary, ask your boss for his help in getting people to do this. E-mail is a great addition to the modern workplace and makes everyone more efficient and independent, including bosses. On balance this is definitely a good thing for assistants; however, you may have to work hard to keep yourself informed and involved (see chapter 12 on being a manager).

Outgoing E-mail

- **When you're composing e-mail memos, make them as professional as you would a paper memo.** Of course, one of the benefits of e-mail is its speed and informality; however, you'll be judged by your e-mails just as you'll be judged by your phone manner and face-to-face communication. Keep your e-mails as short as possible, and get to the point in the first sentence. If you're writing an e-mail to someone outside your company, don't rely upon Word Wrap to set the right margin because it's calculated differently on different programs, and often your memo will appear disjointed to the receiver. Decide upon a margin width for your memo and manually create the margin by hitting Enter to create end of lines. Chat room modes of communication such as abbreviations ("LOL," "BTW," "IMHO"), and emoticons (smiley faces and winking faces) are *not* appropriate in your professional e-mail correspondence.

- **Your e-mail account at work isn't your own.** It belongs to your company and isn't private. You'll use your e-mail to stay in touch with your friends and family, just as you do the telephone in your office, and this is usually expected. But use some caution. Just as you must not chat on the telephone with friends, don't write long e-mails to friends during the workday. And be careful that the e-mails you send to friends within the company and outside the company aren't offensive or indiscreet. Your company can and will monitor your e-mail messages, and you can be fired—or at best, extremely embarrassed—by what you write and send via e-mail.

- **When you get information off the Internet, and a site asks for your e-mail address, give a fake one.** Often a site will request your e-mail address in exchange for letting you get information off their site. If you don't need the site to send you something in return (such as a confirmation), it's easy to give them an inaccurate e-mail address and stop them from sending you junk e-mail. Simply change or delete one letter in your e-mail address when typing it in. You'll still get access to the site, but the computer won't be able to send you anything in the future.

- **Don't sabotage your e-mail readability** by sending out unnecessary or overly long e-mails. If you get a reputation for sending e-mails that are too long or unnecessary, people will delete your e-mails without even opening them.

- **As a courtesy to your reader, don't leave the subject line empty.** Always fill it out with something pertinent to the subject and recognizable to the person receiving the e-mail.

- **Clean up e-mails** that have been going back and forth for a long time and make them comprehensible. Often an e-mail exchange can go on for several pages over many days, and it becomes increasingly difficult to keep track of the discussion and the latest comment. Go ahead and delete old parts of the conversation, and cut and paste sentences which you are responding to. Remember that everyone with an e-mail account is responding to many, many e-mail messages on different subjects (as well as responding to other forms of communication) during a typical day and your electronic conversation is not the only one they have to keep track of.

- **When someone sends you an e-mail, pay attention to the line that tells you who the memo has been sent to before you consider forwarding it on to other people.** Don't forward it to someone who has already received it; this will annoy people and won't win you any friends.

- **Be aware that using block capitals indicates that you're screaming,** and while sometimes this might be appropriate or even necessary, you don't want to do it by accident.

- **It's not usually wise to use the blind carbon copy feature** on your e-mail system. This feature allows you to send an e-mail to someone whose name doesn't appear on the distribution list. If you're doing this because you're trying to do something behind someone's back, then you shouldn't do it. Doing things behind people's backs at work is always a recipe for disaster. The only good time for you to use the blind carbon copy feature is when you're sending a general e-mail out to a large distribution list (for example, informing everyone on your boss's staff of a staff meeting). With the blind carbon copy feature, the long list of names won't appear and the e-mail will be easier and quicker to read. It will also protect the e-mail addresses of everyone you are sending to from being taken by anyone else on the recipient list; this is particularly important if you are sending an e-mail to a huge list of people who don't know each other.

- **Don't use exotic fonts and colors.** They will make your e-mail correspondence difficult and annoying to read.

- **Limit the distribution of your e-mails.** In a busy office, employees will receive up to a hundred e-mails a day, and sifting through them takes a lot of time. Make sure that you're sending e-mail to people that actually need to receive it.

- **Be aware that sending large attachments will tie up the e-mail system, and slow down the accounts of everyone at**

the company. If you have something to send which is extremely large, or contains a lot of graphics and images, check with the computer support team before attaching it and sending it via e-mail.

I recently heard a funny and cautionary story about not paying attention to who your e-mails are going to. An assistant sent an e-mail out to his entire company of six thousand employees when it was supposed to be sent to the employees of only one department. The assistant merely checked the wrong box (mistake number one). The e-mail was received by an employee in the Middle East who decided to respond angrily to the e-mail demanding to know: Why the h*ll it had been sent to him? What idiot was in charge? And was anyone in charge? etc. (mistake number two). The employee in the Middle East clicked "reply to all" so his angry mail went back to the entire distribution list of all six thousand employees instead of just the sender (mistake number three). And for some reason that no one can explain, the employee sent his angry response to the distribution list five times (mistake number four). Not only is this a warning about causing yourself embarrassment due to a lack of attention to details, it involves a more serious warning. The entire computer system crashed at the company because it couldn't handle the volume of e-mails being (unnecessarily) sent. Neither the assistant nor the employee in the Middle East was formally reprimanded for their mistakes; however, over a year later the screwup is still what they are both best known for at the company and it has caused them a lot of embarrassment.

- **A good rule is to not send an e-mail that you have written at the end of the day if you're angry or tired,** but wait until the next morning and reread it. Usually after a night's sleep you will want to edit what you've written and be more diplomatic or clear.

- **Get back to people quickly.** Let them know their e-mail was received and that you will respond in full as soon as possible. Remember that sending an e-mail is like sending something into a black hole. Unless you use the feature on your program that tells you when the receiver has opened your e-mail, you don't know if it's been received, opened, and read. A quick response confirming receipt—even if you can't get the information the sender has requested right away—will be appreciated.

Security Issues

There are a lot of security issues involving computers and e-mail and you should ask someone in the computer support department at your company to review security guidelines with you. (Computer support departments can also be called "IT," "MIS," or "Tech Support.") If you don't have a computer support department, use your common sense. Here are a few general guidelines:

- **Watch out for attachments;** computer viruses travel and contaminate computers through attachments. Don't open attachments unless you know who sent the e-mail and what the attachment is about. Often a virus travels by getting into one computer and sending itself out to everyone on that computer's e-mail address list, so in fact the person whose name is listed as the sender didn't actually send you the e-mail. Usually e-mails carrying viruses have tantalizing and stupid names meant to draw you in, like: "Want to Have Better Sex?!?!?!," but some virus writers are more sneaky and include attachments with businesslike names, so be careful. You can't spread a virus unless you open the attachment. (It is a common misconception that viruses can be spread by simply opening an e-mail which contains an attachment carrying a virus.) The extension names on an attached file (the part after the dot) can sometimes give you a clue that it might be a virus; you should be suspicious of "exe," "vbs," "Ink," and "ini."

- **Don't walk away from your computer with a document open on your screen.** Imagine that you're typing a memo for your boss regarding upcoming layoffs at the company and you get a call that your boss's lunch is waiting in the reception area. While you run out to get the boss's food and deliver it to him, anyone might pass by your desk and see the memo. And someone doesn't have to be a snoop intentionally looking for information to read your screen. Someone could be dropping something by your desk when the word "layoffs" catches her eye, and she can't help but take a second look at your computer screen.

- **Of course, there are people in the workplace who are intentional snoops and even criminally minded.** You shouldn't leave your computer running while you're away for any length of time because you're giving someone access to its files—it's no different than leaving your apartment unlocked and the door open while you go to the gym. There is a common function on computers which allows you to require a password to wake up a sleeping computer from its screen saver. Again, ask the computer tech guys about this.

- **Don't leave computer disks and CDs lying around** where they might be stolen. They're small and easy to take and conceal.

- **Create a strong password** for your computer to make it harder to break into. There are software packages designed to discover a password. A strong password is one that is not an English language word. Use a phrase with a combination of letters and numbers instead. Of course, these are harder to remember so you can play a little trick to help yourself: Think of a statement you can remember easily, such as "Elvis was the rock 'n' roll king." Take the first letter of each word to create your password, "EWTRNRK," and then throw in some numbers to make it a harder code to break. Elvis died in 1977, so: "EWTRNRK77." Another hint: Make your password at least eight characters long.

- **Always back up your files.** Save important files onto a floppy disk and keep it secure. Talk to the computer tech guys about the best way to safeguard your files in case of a major system crash.

Probably every job you will ever have will require strong communications skills, and a big part of this is writing. Consider that all the correspondence you handle in your boss's office, from e-mails to "snail mail" letters, is practice for you. The more you write, the better you will become at expressing your ideas clearly and briefly. So take the time to work on your writing.

chapter 6

Some Bosses Are Jerks, But You Still Have to Talk to Them

Goal: To adapt to your boss's way of communicating. Good communication is critical for a productive working relationship.

What Kind of Boss Do You Have?

Different personalities require different communication styles, and, as the assistant, you must be flexible and adapt to your boss's way of working. Communication can be loose and relaxed with a boss to whom you have a great deal of access or very structured and formal with a less receptive boss. If your boss and your work environment are easygoing, you'll be able to ask your boss questions merely by sticking your head into his office throughout the day. If, however, your boss has a more difficult personality, you'll need to plan your opportunities to talk to him. Bosses are human, and thus have many different characteristics, some negative and some positive. Of course, you'll find that certain characteristics in your boss are more important to you than others. For example: Is he a patient person? Or is he always looking for someone to blame, other than himself? And just as it's possible that you'll work for someone who is mean and spiteful, you also might work for someone who is not very smart. You'll also have to judge your boss's attention span and the best way to get him to take in information. Some people cannot focus on a thick brief of papers, and need to be given information verbally, others need to have information in a short written summary. You have to accommodate yourself to everything in your boss's personality if you are going to stay with him.

Communicating in Writing

During our first weeks as boss and assistant, George communicated with me exclusively through Post-it Notes. I would find them on my phone and desk with instructions to do certain things. I think George found this the easiest way to communicate initially because he wasn't quite sure how to be a boss to an assistant (he'd never had one before), and how to make use of me. I quickly learned that George was very comfortable communicating through paper and writing, and I adapted to this. Over the years we continued to "talk" through paper and made great use of Post-it Notes. If I needed to ask him something, nine times out of ten, I would type it onto paper and put it in front of him or in his in-box, depending upon its urgency, and he would write his response on the same sheet.

This system has benefits for the assistant; you're getting a reasonably thoughtful response because your boss is forced to pay enough attention to read your question. Often a distracted boss will only half listen to your questions asked verbally and give thoughtless responses that he might later regret. By communicating on paper, you also will have your boss's response in writing in case there is ever any question in the future regarding his response and directions. If your boss's directions are written on a Post-it Note, you should staple the Post-it Note to a larger piece of paper so that it doesn't get lost. Since George, I've had another boss that liked to communicate through e-mail, and this had the same benefits of getting a response in writing. I wasn't his assistant (although it could be argued that everyone is their boss's assistant, even if their title is something more grand and they don't answer his phone), and I wasn't in close physical proximity to him; therefore, e-mail was very convenient. If your boss is comfortable with e-mail and checks it often, you should use it as a way to communicate as often as possible.

Some Bosses Can Be Jerks . . .

As I have said, your mode of communication with your boss will depend entirely upon his character; however, your style of communication should also depend on his character. Perhaps you'll be blessed with an opportunity to work for a boss who is fair, even-tempered, and intelligent. If this is the case, you'll be given a chance to communicate easily and naturally with your boss. However, there is the unfortunate chance that your boss will be a nightmare. He will yell and scream at everyone who works for him and others who don't, he will assign blame indiscriminately but never accept it himself, he'll never say thank you, and will never, ever treat you with respect. Most bosses who are nightmares to work for are smart and sophisticated, and they know that they're jerks to everyone who works for them, particularly their assistants. To keep you from quitting, they'll often compensate for their behavior by paying you a good salary and buying you gifts. They'll also do something common in abusive relationships; they'll counter their inexcusable behavior with moments of charm, high praise, and affection. Successful, powerful people who have assistants are people who are very skilled at interpersonal manipulation. Of course, this is a worst-case scenario, and most bosses are regular people who have good days and bad days.

My friend Luke attended a daylong presentation at his company in which each team reported on their progress on their projects to the entire department of thirty people, their immediate boss, and the boss's boss. A guy named Sam was giving his presentation when the big boss interrupted him and calmly said: "It's clear this project is an utter disaster, and I can tell why." Sam was stunned into silence and the big boss stood up, pointed at him, and began shouting at the top of his lungs: "I've never seen a project so far in the s**t, and only a stupid, incompetent f***er like you, Sam, could create such a f***ing disaster for us! I can't believe we ever even hired you! You have got to be one of the most f***ing idiotic, incompetent people in this organization!" Then it got even worse as the department head, who had been working with Sam on his presentation joined in: "He's right, Sam, I can't believe it either. You've taken this project in completely the wrong direction, and I've never thought you were competent either!" Obviously, the big boss was a bully, but the department head was even worse: He was a coward and a bully. Luke told me that the morale of the department never recovered after that incident and eventually his boss was fired because he couldn't manage his own staff. (Sam still works there).

How to Handle a Jerk

If you have a boss who is a nightmare, you must first ask yourself if it's really worth it to you to work for this person and be abused. If the answer is "yes," then here are a few tips.

- **Your self-esteem is going to take a severe beating; make sure that you have a support system.** Talk to friends and family. You'll need to get affirmations from them. You might have some pangs of guilt for being indiscreet and telling stories, particularly unflattering ones, about your boss. But in my opinion your boss lost his right to your silent loyalty when he became abusive, and self-survival is more important. However, do choose the people you talk to carefully. I recommend you talk to friends and family who don't work in your industry; if it gets back to your boss that you're talking about him, he'll probably fire you.

- **Don't let your boss see that he's getting to you.** Bullies are like wolves, they go straight for the weak and lame and slaughter them. This means that you must not cry in front of your boss—go to the bathroom.

- **Don't shout back at your boss.** It will only increase his anger. Although I do know people who have used shouting back at a boss as a shock technique and it has worked, it's a risky thing to try. And anyway, even if it worked due to shock value, it would only work once or twice.

- **Try to set boundaries.** Tell your boss that yelling at you isn't acceptable. This won't stop him from yelling at you, but if you are a confident person and you stand up to your boss, he might respect you for it and you'll feel less like a doormat. Be warned though, a real bully will see this as fighting back and it will cause him to fight harder in an effort to dominate you.

Denise had a boss once who routinely shouted: "Hey, You! Hey, You!" across the room at her to get her attention. Denise pointedly ignored her until she called to her by name, or came over to her desk. The boss couldn't chastise Denise for ignoring her because her own behavior was so awful. This same boss once introduced Denise to a client as: "Whatever your name is . . ." The interesting epilogue to these stories is that they happened a long time ago and Denise, who is now an executive at a production company, is professionally friendly with her old boss. She recently teased her about her rude behavior, and Denise's former boss was indignant and swore that she had never acted like that. The point is that if they can be made aware of their unacceptable behavior, some bosses will shape up.

- **Be very good at your job and don't make mistakes.** This way you're creating insurance against your boss yelling at you. If you don't make mistakes he'll have fewer reasons to be abusive. Create a paper trail, and get everything in writing. If he blames you for things having gone wrong, you'll have proof that you acted as he instructed.

The Control Freak

The good news is that most control freak bosses will relax somewhat as time passes and they grow to trust you more and more. But if your boss is overcontrolling, and it's not because you are totally inexperienced or making a lot of mistakes, there are a few ways of handling the situation.

- **Give your boss tons of written information.** This will have two effects: It will make him feel more confident that you are doing a thorough job and he will be overwhelmed by the amount of paper and will just leave you alone to do your work.

- **Say to your boss: "I don't want to waste your time.** Why don't you give me a day or two to come up with some proposals to show you and then I can get your input?"

- **Don't ask your boss for his advice or opinions.** This is a dangerous option and you should only do this if you are 100 percent confident that you know what you are doing and that you won't make any mistakes. If you do complete a task without his input, make sure that you create a paper trail so that if (when) your boss questions what you did you can show him step by step.

What If Your Boss Is Wrong?

Another difficult type of boss to work for is one who is a fool. You'll have to make careful decisions as to whether it's prudent for you to correct your boss when he's wrong. The best way to handle this is to offer your boss different (better) solutions to a problem, and if necessary to give him the correct information. Make sure that you do this in a nonthreatening way though; people don't like to be told they're wrong, particularly by someone who is their junior. If you make your boss look stupid, believe me, he will be smart enough to get rid of you so that he no longer looks stupid.

The same Denise whom I mentioned earlier was working at a public relations firm and her boss (not the one mentioned earlier) was organizing a fund-raising dinner for the Animal Rescue Fund of New York. Denise saw the planned menu the day of the event, and felt compelled to tell her boss that veal was not the best choice for the main course. Another time Denise was in a meeting with the same boss discussing the timing of a publicity event. The choices were during Fashion Week or during the Olympics. The boss said: "Well, nobody watches the Olympics!" Denise decided to tell her boss, a socialite from Manhattan, that where she came from a lot of people actually watched the Olympics. In both cases, my friend presented her correction of her boss in a nonthreatening way. For example, she might have said: "You couldn't be expected to know this, Mary, because you lead a very glamorous life here in Manhattan, but I believe that a lot of people in the rest of the country do watch the Olympics. I know my family in Kansas City does. Would you like me to get you the ratings for the Olympics over the past ten years so we have some facts to work with?"

James recruits college graduates for his company, which has revenues of over $7 billion a year. He had to tell his boss that the scheduled interviews with the candidates he had picked would be delayed because all the hotels in the area were booked. His boss suggested that instead of delaying the interviews, my friend could put the candidates up at his house, sleeping on the couch and floor, and he could drive them into the office in the morning. James told his boss that he thought that wouldn't be fair to his family, and besides, it might not give the right impression for a major multinational corporation.

It Comes Down to This

You were hired because you're smart, and if you can save your boss from making a bad decision, do it. But be careful *how* you do it, and don't feel hurt if he reacts less than graciously to being corrected.

Simon is the press officer for the well-known head of a media company, and the boss is known to be difficult, to say the least. He was in the middle of conducting a press conference with Simon at his side, and he gave the press some wrong information. Simon told him of his mistake under his breath, and the boss turned to him and said in a normal tone of voice: "F*** off." Simon, who has worked for this man for years, and gets paid a lot of money, just took a step backward and laughed about it later with all his friends in the press.

Meetings—Be Prepared

Regardless of how you manage communication with your boss, meetings with him are crucial. Your goal should be to have daily meetings both first and last thing every day, longer weekly meetings, and progress reviews every two to three months. Go into every meeting with your boss prepared; have your questions written down in your notebook in order of importance and stick to your list. Make sure that you anticipate questions that your boss will ask you in response to your questions to him. For example: When you go into your meeting with your boss and you ask him if he'd like to attend the meeting in San Diego of

Black Congressional Members which he has been invited to, be prepared for your boss to ask what time the meeting will start and other logistical questions. If there is a written invitation, have it in your hand to show to him, if he asks to see it. Be prepared with flight information to and from San Diego and his current schedule for the day of the meeting: for example, "There is a direct flight at 8 A.M. that would get you into San Diego at 9 A.M. and you could be back to the office by 2 P.M. You would miss the weekly marketing meeting, and our sales team from Europe will be visiting the office that day." Your boss needs to know what time commitment the event would require due to traveling and what meetings he would miss at the office so that he can make an informed decision about attending the event.

My friend Patricia told me that her assistant comes into her office to ask if she wants to attend an event and doesn't know anything about the logistics of the event. When Patricia asks to see the invitation, so she can do her assistant's job for her and find out the logistics, the assistant invariably replies: "You have it." The assistant should have located the invitation in her boss's office before the meeting; in fact, the invitation should never have been left in her boss's office in the first place. Before you walk into your boss's office, make sure that you have everything you need to show or give to him—you don't want to waste your boss's time as you run back to your desk for something you forgot.

More About Meetings

In reality, you may find that you'll meet far less than twice daily, weekly, and bimonthly, especially if you're competent and your boss is happy with your work. Your meeting time will be the first thing to be sacrificed on the schedule if the schedule changes during the day. And because you're always there, your boss will always feel like the meeting can be put off until later if he isn't in the mood to meet with you. Since you manage your boss's schedule, you get to decide when to schedule your own meetings with your boss, so don't undermine yourself—make sure they occur at a time when you'll get his attention, and he'll be in the most receptive mood. Be familiar with your boss's attention span. Don't try to give him too much information if you know he has a tendency to get bored and stop paying attention. If he does have a short attention span, schedule several very short meetings of five minutes during his office time over a period of a couple of days. If you know that something is going on and that your boss will be distracted, and you don't have anything urgent to report, cancel your own meeting. Likewise, if you don't have anything important to tell him, cancel your meeting. Do not waste his time.

Face Time

Meetings are important "face time" for you with your boss and you must create a good impression. Bosses hate these meetings; they bore them and they often think they are a waste of their time. Again, make sure you don't waste your boss's time. Be well prepared with a list of objectives for the meeting. Don't ramble, get to the point, and don't overburden your boss with information he doesn't need. Give him the minimal amount of information necessary; he'll ask you to elaborate if he needs to know more. Make sure you aren't just complaining to him and telling him your problems in getting your work done. You must prioritize your questions in case time runs out with your boss; always work off an "A" list of objectives and a "B" list of objectives.

* * *

Priorities will change as things happen throughout the day—your questions will become more or less urgent and you need to be sensitive to this. Early in the 1992 Clinton campaign, before the creation of the War Room, George traveled with the governor on the campaign trail. He would call our office at the headquarters in Little Rock at least once a day for his phone messages. On campaigns there is a great schism between the campaign headquarters and the "plane" (shorthand for the team traveling with the candidate on the campaign trail). The plane thinks the headquarters is largely obsolete, and the headquarters spends a lot of time trying to prove it isn't. (Of course, both are essential.) In a typical plane versus headquarters situation, George didn't call into the office as often as I thought he should, and when he did, he became quickly impatient with my list of objectives for our call because the issues we were dealing with at the headquarters, which seemed important to us, seemed unimportant to George, who was with the candidate and on a very tight schedule. I learned to prioritize, and keep my questions and information to an absolute minimum. I had an A list of information and questions for him and a B list, and I bluntly asked him which he had time for. Since I never knew when he would call in, I had to keep amending my A list and B list, moving things from one to the other as their priority changed, and constantly be prepared to update George on what was happening in Little Rock.

Daily Meetings

Daily meetings should be quick: no more than fifteen minutes, first thing in the morning and last thing in the evening. This is an opportunity to talk about the day's (or next day's) schedule and any questions you have regarding it, phone calls to be returned, and anything on your to-do list that requires your boss's attention.

Weekly Meetings

Weekly meetings will be a little longer than daily meetings and should be your opportunity to get and receive less timely information. If you have a good rapport with your boss, these meetings should be more relaxed than your daily meetings. You can go over incoming scheduling requests and projects you're working on. This is also your chance to ask questions to educate yourself.

Bimonthly Meetings

Meetings every two to three months will give you a chance to get a performance review from your boss, and let him know of any problems you're having with your job. This is a great time to discuss your long-term career goals. The best way to approach this is through flattery. I know it sounds silly, but truthfully all bosses like to be flattered by their employees. The great thing about flattery is that people believe it. You can say almost anything—no matter how far from the truth it might be—and they will want to believe it if it flatters them. However, stick to the truth if possible. Compliment them on things you honestly do admire and bring yourself into the conversation. For example: "George, I was really impressed with how you handled that reporter's question on Bosnia. I hope I can be a press secretary one day. How did you learn to answer reporters questions so seemingly effortlessly?" Don't be self-conscious, because even though a smart boss will know you are flattering him, he won't care, he'll still enjoy it and probably will think you're very perceptive. Once you have opened a line of conversation and warmed up your boss with flattery, start to mention your own goals and aspirations.

Making Mistakes

You'll make mistakes. Be upfront about it. Trying to cover up an error is foolish and will only make you look worse when it is discovered, which is inevitable. As soon as you discover a mistake you've made, let your boss know and tell him what you are doing to rectify the mistake. Be as truthful, forthcoming, and blunt as possible.

However, you need to realize that there are mistakes that you can fix and there's no need to tell your boss about, and there are others that will have far-reaching implications which you must own up to. Understanding the difference requires judgment and common sense. For example: If you call in figures to the agency preparing your company's annual report and a few hours later realize you called in the wrong set of numbers, you can simply call back the agency and correct your own mistake. There's no need to tell your boss what you did. But if you don't catch your mistake and the proof of the book arrives with the wrong numbers laid out in type, then you need to own up to your boss that you made a mistake. Point it out to him (if he hasn't already caught it) and tell him you'll get the agency on the phone and ask them to put together a new proof as soon as possible. Why do you need to admit your mistake? Because you will have cost the company money and the proof of the annual report will arrive later than expected. And in most practical terms because you will be found out.

The most important thing to remember about making mistakes at work is that it is very, very unlikely that you will be fired because of your mistake. Every employee makes mistakes. If you made an honest mistake while trying to do the right thing (as opposed to making the "mistake" of trying to cheat on your expense account) the absolute worst-case scenario is that your boss will be mad, you will be reprimanded, and your mistake will be recorded in your personnel file. But this is the absolute worst-case scenario; more than likely your boss will simply tell you to fix the mistake.

chapter 7

"How's Never? Is Never Good for You?" Keeping a Schedule

Goal: To make your boss as efficient as possible by managing her time well.

What Type Is Your Boss?

You'll be managing your boss's time, and you must make the most of it. This doesn't mean filling her days with endless meetings; you have to accommodate your boss's work style. Does she have lots of energy in the morning or later in the afternoon? How busy is she willing to be? Is she always late? You must schedule downtime when she's traveling (personal time on the schedule for her to relax). And every day you must schedule office time, during which she can go through her paperwork and return important phone calls.

Schedules Change Constantly

The schedule will change constantly throughout the day. Don't get upset if it seems all your work is wasted as a meeting you spent days setting up is canceled. Just mentally move on, cancel the meeting, and reschedule it for another day. As an assistant, you have to be flexible, which means being willing and able to make changes quickly. Unfortunately, it's easy to get frustrated as the schedule changes, and you not only see your work wasted, but more work created—especially if it seems to you that the schedule is changing because of your boss's capriciousness. However, do not allow your frustration to make you rigid and angry, just let it go. The schedule is going to change. It is the nature of a busy executive to be needed in multiple places at one time, and as priorities change so will the schedule you have put together. You'll get used to calling people and explaining that your boss has to change her schedule, and therefore their meeting is canceled or postponed. Be gracious, and apologetic—just imagine the work that they did to prepare for the meeting you're canceling—but never criticize your boss for the changing schedule out of frustration.

Coordinating Schedules

Unless your boss is the ultimate head of the company for which you work, the chances are you'll need to coordinate your boss's schedule with her boss's schedule. When I worked for George, I always kept a copy of the president's daily and long-term schedule in my bible (see chapter 3). Of course, the president's schedule would change constantly and George's schedule changed with it. Many of the events, trips, and meetings on the president's schedule involved George, so I put them immediately onto his schedule. But what was more complicated was predicting when George would be needed by the president and called into the Oval Office. The worst situation was having George out of the White House, and the president requesting him in the Oval. Obviously if he was in the White House I could pull him out of a meeting for the president, but if he was across town, unless I could get him on the phone (which was never satisfactory), he failed at his most important duty—being at the beck and call of the president.

With experience you'll know when your boss will need to be available to another principal, and you'll be able to look at the schedule of your boss's boss and predict times she'll need to be available. One trick is to try to mirror the schedule of your boss's boss: Schedule your boss's office time at the same time as that of her boss, and schedule her to be out of the office when her boss is out too. This is an example of when you need to have a good relationship with your coworkers to do your job well: You should be on great terms with the assistant of your boss's boss. She can help you out a lot—or make your life difficult—because you'll need information from her. If she respects and trusts you, then you should have no trouble getting the information you need to coordinate your boss's schedule.

Ask Questions and Plan

Don't make assumptions about the schedule; ask your boss questions until you learn how she likes to work. Depending upon the timing of the scheduling questions, plan to ask these in an organized way at one time, probably at your daily or weekly meetings (see chapter 6). When you plan to talk to your boss about the schedule, give yourself time to:

1) Meet with your boss and ask questions
2) Let your boss think about her answers to your questions and get back to you
3) Make whatever plans are necessary

Don't wait to talk to your boss about something on the schedule until the last minute because you'll have to rush to get answers and force her to make decisions. Then you'll be scrambling to make plans. Panic can usually be avoided by good planning. I once saw a sign above someone's desk that said: "Lack of planning on your part does not constitute an emergency on my part." Make sure you don't create emergencies by your lack of planning; your boss, and circumstances beyond anyone's control, will create enough scheduling emergencies without you adding to them.

Adapt to Your Boss's Schedule

When your boss travels out of town and into another time zone, you should change your schedule to accommodate her. For example, if you are based in Los Angeles, and your boss is working in New York for three days, sorry, but you need to be at the office in Los Angeles on East Coast time (three hours earlier). The good news is that you can go home earlier, but not until your boss's workday is finished (including making sure she gets to a business dinner with no problems).

Calendars

There are two main elements to scheduling, the daily and the long-term calendars. You'll keep three calendars, a month-at-a-view calendar, and two week-at-a-view desk diaries—one for your boss and one for you.

- **Month-at-a-View**—(page 110) Use a computer program. Print out the next two or three months and keep them in the bible (see chapter 3) for quick reference. You can make changes to the calendar by hand on the printout, and then update it in the computer at the end of the day. Travel, events, all-day meetings, and anything else that blocks out several hours of your boss's day should go on this calendar. Put everything on this calendar that your boss might attend, including events for which you haven't sent an RSVP.

- **Your Week-at-a-View**—Use a desk diary. Keep your own schedule here, both personal and professional. This is an important habit for you to get into for when you are no longer an assistant. This is where you'll put reminders to yourself to call and get confirmations for a meeting you have scheduled, to pick up your boss's black tie outfit for an event the next night, or any other reminders you need.

- **Boss's Week-at-a-View**—(page 111) Again, use a desk diary, and write in pencil. Put everything on this calendar, no matter how small or large, and cross-reference with the month-at-a-view calendar to make sure that nothing is forgotten. At the end of every day, type up the schedule for the next day and print it out. Make a small pocket-sized copy for your boss (George kept his daily schedule in his suit jacket breast pocket (see page 112), and print out a copy for the bible (see chapter 3). You'll have to make updates throughout the day as the schedule changes, and reprint copies. Make sure that you put the time the new version is generated at the top of the schedule so that neither you nor your boss gets confused. I always wrote it in red pen at the top. Your boss might use a Palm Pilot, or another brand of electronic personal organizer. If she does, then you'll need to learn how to download her schedule onto it from your computer instead of giving her paper copies of her schedule. As you plan your boss's day don't forget to plan in travel time to and from meetings (even meetings within your office building), time for meetings to run overtime, time to eat, and office time to return phone calls and e-mails, and do paperwork.

Below is an example of a month-at-a-view calendar for George while we worked at the White House.

March

Sun	Mon	Tue	Wed	Thu	Fri	Sat
		1 T.H.I.S Event	**2** Dinner w/ Sen. Feingold	**3** POTUS trip to San Diego	**4** POTUS Radio Address	**5**
6 Mtg. Black Congressional Members	**7** White House State Dinner	**8**	**9** Teach for America Event	**10** Brown Bag Lunch/Talk @ Dept. of Interior	**11** POTUS Radio Address	**12**
13 Tree of Life Awards (Ohio)	**14** Dinner for Rahm's Birthday	**15**	**16** Roast: Tim Russert	**17** Florida Greek Festival	**18** POTUS Radio Address	**19**
20	**21** Greek-American Community Service Awards (NYC)	**22**	**23** Movie Opening	**24**	**25** POTUS Radio Address	**26**
27 Larry King's B-day	**28**	**29** Women in Media Awards Dinner	**30** Dinner with Newsweeklies	**31** POTUS Radio Address		

Below is an example of a page from the desk diary I kept for George while we were at the White House.

MONDAY	TUESDAY	WEDNESDAY	THURSDAY	FRIDAY	SATURDAY	SUNDAY
8 A.M. Senior Staff Mtg.	**8 A.M.** Senior Staff Mtg.	**8 A.M.** Senior Staff Mtg.	**8 A.M.** Senior Staff Mtg.	**8 A.M.** Senior Staff Mtg.	**9 A.M.** Presidential Radio Address	
10 A.M. Secret Service Briefing	**8:30** NEC mtg.	**9 A.M.** POTUS Mtg. re. Health Care	**10:30** Cabinet Mtg. w/POTUS	**9:45** Mtg. with COS, Tyson, Sen. Bentson		
11 A.M. POTUS interview with NY Times	**10:30** Strategy Mtg.	**11:30** Photo Shoot with Rick Bloom		**11:30** NSC Mtg. in Situation Room		
Lunch with William Safire at The Palm		Lunch with Walter Isaacson				
2:30 Mtg. on NAFTA		**2:15 P.M.** POTUS Mtg. re. Gun Control	**2 P.M.** Interview with Mark Miller	**2 P.M.** Elton John at WH		
		4:45 Interview with London Sunday Times		**4–6 P.M.** drop by baby shower for Bruce Reed		
	6 P.M. Political Mtg.					
Party for Gephardt	Dinner with Mark Halperin	Dinner with Harold	Dinner with James C.	Dinner with Paul & Family		

Below is an example of a daily schedule for George. I would create these and print them out the night before for the next day. I printed my copy on 8 1/2" x 11" paper and kept it in my bible (see chapter 3). I printed George's copy on 3" x 6" cards that fit into his jacket's breast pocket. The example below is about actual size; I would print on both sides of the card.

THE WHITE HOUSE
George Stephanopoulos

Friday, 05.27.94

8:00 A.M.	Senior Staff Mtg. Roosevelt Room
9 A.M.	Office Time
10 A.M.– 10:15 A.M.	POTUS Economic Briefing, OVAL
10:15 A.M.	Office Time
10:45 A.M.– 11:45 A.M.	POTUS Planning Mtg. with HRC Map Room
12:00 P.M.	Health Care Mtg.
12:30 P.M.	Harold's Office

FYI: 12 P.M. D-Day Scheduling
Mtg. 180 OEOB

12:30 P.M.	Depart White House
12:40 P.M.	Lunch with E. Drew Hay Adams Hotel
1:30 P.M.	Depart Hay Adams
1:40 P.M.	Arrive White House
Continued . . .	

Scheduling Meetings

The most prevalent item on your boss's schedule will be meetings. Your boss will be asked to attend endless meetings, and until you understand her job well, you'll have to ask her which meetings she wants to attend. Don't ask her every time a call comes in with a request for her attendance at a meeting; plan to ask these questions at either your daily or weekly meetings (see chapter 6). You'll also be asked to schedule meetings for your boss. Until you have more experience, you will need to ask your boss for direction in scheduling meetings for her. The following are the things you need to be concerned with as you schedule a meeting. Plan to ask these questions during your meetings with her, unless she has the time to give you the information you need when she tells you to put the meeting together.

• **Who are the participants and what are their titles and affiliations?** You need to understand the food chain—who is the most important person on the list, and whose attendance at the meeting is crucial. The meeting's time and location will be scheduled to accommodate this person. Who are the lower-level participants on the list? They can be expected to change their schedule to accommodate the meeting. Are there participants who will be expected to make a presentation at the meeting or have materials prepared? Make sure you let them know about the meeting as soon as possible; the more you can help other members of your boss's staff do their jobs well, the more they'll like you. Obviously, the more they like you, the more they'll help you do a good job. It's important to remember that if you get promoted within your boss's department, you'll be working with or for his staff. If you aren't helpful to them now and if you don't protect them from your boss when necessary, they'll remember it.

• Location—Meetings always occur in the place most convenient to the most powerful person attending the meeting. Keep a list of possible locations for meetings such as restaurants, conference rooms within your building, and hotel conference rooms with contact names and phone numbers on the list. Do you need audio or video equipment set up for the meeting? Do you need to cater food for the meeting?

- **Time, date, and probable duration.**

- **Subject**—Make sure you truly understand the reason for the meeting, so that you can tell the participants you'll be inviting. If you're even slightly unclear as to the subject of the meeting, or a project as a whole, ask your boss to explain it to you. Ask her at a moment when she has the time to explain it to you without getting annoyed, perhaps during your weekly meeting. You need to genuinely understand what your boss is working on because this is how you learn. That's why you have this job—to learn. It's important to really understand because other people will be able to tell if you have no idea what is going on, and they'll treat you accordingly. If people know that you have answers and information, they'll start coming to you for help because it will be easier to get to you than to your boss, and this is how you can expand your role as assistant. If, on the other hand, they know that you don't really understand a project, they'll simply use you to take messages for your boss.

- **Confirmations**—After you have worked with the assistants to the most important participants and come up with a date, time, and location, you'll call or e-mail all the participants and ask them to put the meeting on their schedules. Mark your desk diary with a reminder the day before the meeting to call the participants and confirm their attendance, and to call and confirm the room you have booked for the meeting; also confirm any special items such as food or equipment.

- **Agenda**—(below) Most meetings of more than two people that aren't regularly scheduled meetings require an agenda, which states the major points that will be discussed at the meeting. It's considerate to distribute copies of the agenda before the meeting so that everyone comes prepared (e-mail is great for this). Extra copies of the agenda need to be available at the meeting because people will forget to bring it with them. Are you responsible for the agenda, or is another member of your boss's staff? If it's someone else's responsibility, call him and make sure he knows all the details of the meeting. If it's your responsibility and you've never written one, ask someone for assistance. The best person would be someone on your boss's staff who will be attending the meeting and who is nice. If this person doesn't exist, ask another assistant to an executive. Regardless of your experience, give a draft of the agenda to your boss to edit before the meeting. Agendas can be very political in terms of who speaks when, and what is discussed, and you don't want to make a mistake.

Below is an example of an agenda for a meeting.

February 8, 2001
TO: Mary Brown, Joe Smith, Bill Clarke, Jim Shelton, Liz Peton, Sam Scout
FR: Heather Beckel
RE: Agenda for Meeting on Fund-raising Efforts

- Review of current financial situation (Jim Shelton)
- Review of last fund-raising drive (Joe Smith)
- Ideas for next fund-raising drive (group discussion)
- Update on status of database of possible donors (Bill Clarke)
- Assignments and goals for next meeting (Mary Brown)

Travel Schedules

When your boss tells you about a trip she'll be taking, the first thing you must do is block out the dates on both your calendars (Month-at-a-View and the Week-at-a-View). To begin scheduling travel for your boss, start a working schedule; work backward and forward from the reason for trip. For example: Your boss is going to Cleveland to tour a factory and the tour is on Tuesday from 10 A.M. to 12 P.M. Put that on the schedule, and then determine how long it will take to get from the airport to the factory (ask your contact at the factory in Cleveland); determine if there are any flights that get into Cleveland early enough in the morning to get to the factory by 10 A.M. Let's suppose that there is a flight departing at 6 A.M. that would get her to Cleveland in time for the tour—you have your first question for your boss: Would she like to catch the 6 A.M. flight or would she prefer to travel the night before and stay overnight in Cleveland? Start a list of questions regarding this trip, keep it in your notebook, and try to ask your boss all the questions you have regarding this trip at one time during one of your meetings. Then work forward from the time the tour ends; would your boss like to have lunch with someone from the factory or does she want to leave Cleveland as soon as possible? Keep the working travel schedule in your bible (see chapter 3), and make notes on it of all telephone numbers and confirmation numbers that pertain to the trip. Don't forget to schedule downtime for your boss while she is traveling. "Downtime" is personal time on the schedule for her to relax. Don't trust the people who your boss is traveling to see to take care of her arrangements for you, or, if you do, double-check their work. If something goes wrong, she won't complain to them—she'll be on the phone screaming at you (the nicest boss will become tense when she's traveling and her schedule gets screwed up).

I once scheduled a speaking engagement in Miami for George while he was President Clinton's senior advisor. He was met at the airport by a white stretch limo. The organization that he was visiting was honored to have someone of George's stature as their speaker, and they wanted to treat him as well as they possibly could. To them, a white stretch limo was the best ground transportation available, and fitting to George's importance as they saw it. However, at the time, the press was especially critical of George for what it characterized as his youthful arrogance, and George was horrified that someone would see him getting into the flashy limo, which would play into the current opinion of him. I learned the importance of confirming and reviewing every detail on a schedule, and not trusting anyone else with organizing my boss's arrangements.

Airlines, Ground Transportation, and Hotels

Although expectations vary from industry to industry and company to company, everywhere I've ever worked, both in the public and private sectors, assistants were expected to organize both the boss's professional *and* personal travel plans. You'll need to understand the differences in the way she travels depending on whether she or the company is paying for the trip. The following are the major elements of scheduling a trip, either personal or professional; use these to formulate the questions you'll have to ask your boss as you plan a trip.

- **Airlines**—Which are your boss's favorite airlines and which does she refuse to travel on? She'll have frequent flyer memberships for most airlines (but if she doesn't, you should get them for her), and she'll probably prefer to travel on the airlines with which she has accrued the most mileage. Keep a file with her membership numbers listed and the number of miles she has accrued with each airline. You'll need a good travel agent and you must cultivate a great relationship with him or her. Send them presents whenever possible, and treat them with respect—you'll be asking them for lots of last-minute favors as your boss's schedule changes. Good travel agents can create miracles, and they have lots of goodies to give away if they like you—like upgrades to first class. You need to know the type of seating your boss prefers and if she has any special food requests (you can request special meals on airlines in any class, such as low-calorie, kosher, vegetarian, and so forth). Executives and VIPs do not travel like the rest of us; there are special waiting lounges for people who travel in business or first class. They are quiet with comfortable seating, and offer special services, such as showers, fitness centers, ports for computers, and fax machines. If your boss isn't traveling business or first class, you can get access to these waiting lounges in one of three other ways: with a certain number of frequent flyer miles, by paying an annual fee, or by asking your travel agent if he has this perk to offer your boss. The luxury of these waiting lounges can really make a difference in the stress level of a busy traveler. Airports also have departments called Special Services, which offer just that, special services to traveling VIPs. Their job is to do such things as move celebrity travelers quickly through the public areas of the airport, check them in without waiting in line, offer them security, and get their luggage off the plane quickly. You also need to understand your company's restrictions on travel, such as what class your boss is allowed to travel (most companies determine whether an employee can travel first class, business class, or coach based on their rank at the company and the length of the flight). Always ask your travel agent for several options of flights, but try to get the most direct flights, or those with the shortest layovers.

- **Ground transportation**—Generally speaking you'll want to schedule a car service for your boss when she's traveling for business. All major U.S. cities have taxis, but in some cities they have to be called for by telephone because they aren't available to hail on the street. And even if taxis are available to hail on the street, finding one when you need it can be unreliable. Not to mention weather constraints: Imagine your boss in a suit on the street trying to find a cab in a snowstorm in Chicago, or in Houston's tropical humidity. Another negative point about using taxis on business trips is that your boss will have to carry cash to pay and will have to remember to ask for receipts and not lose them, or you'll not be able to get reimbursements for her. If your boss is traveling for business she should have the luxury and convenience of a car service at her disposal, and it'll make your life easier. Try to use the same car service company every time your boss returns to a city because you'll get better treatment as a returning customer. Having a relationship with them will be very useful when your boss leaves her briefcase in one of their cars. Your boss will call you, in another city, and expect you to retrieve her briefcase and have it delivered to her in the hotel within the hour. Learn what kind of car your boss prefers, and if she will need special services such as a phone or television in the car. Make sure you understand the layout of the city your boss is visiting, and how long it will take to get from point A to point B. See the appendix for this information, ask the car service to help you, or use a Web-based map program to calculate mileage and time between your boss's appointments. Not often, but sometimes, your boss might want to rent a car. Usually this will be when she is traveling to a city she knows very well, when she is staying in one city for an extended period of time, or when she is traveling with one or more other people. Ask your travel agent to assist you in booking a car, and again, they can offer you upgrades. Find out if your company has limits on what they'll pay per day for car rental, and check with your boss on her preferences (if she's going to L.A., she might want a convertible).

- **Hotels**—Keep a list of your boss's hotel preferences in different cities with contact names at the hotel. If your boss is a frequent traveler, the management at the hotel will give her special treatment as a returning guest. Like airlines, hotels have the ability to offer your boss upgrades to better rooms. Before your boss arrives, get the name and direct telephone number of the hotel's concierge. A hotel concierge's job is essentially to take care of your boss while she's staying at the hotel in the way you care for her at home. Traditionally, a concierge will help guests with their luggage, mail, make reservations at local restaurants, arrange tours, etc., but you will find that, if you're charming enough, a good concierge will do almost anything for your boss. He can be a huge asset to you because he's there locally with your boss. For example, after your boss has called you to let you know that she left her briefcase in the car service sedan, call the concierge and tell him what happened and that you're calling the car service. The concierge will watch for the delivery of the briefcase, and make sure that your boss gets it as soon as it arrives. He'll even follow up with the car service, if it hasn't arrived when it was promised. Hopefully your boss will be sophisticated enough to tip everyone at the hotel generously before she leaves, because this will make your job much easier. Unfortunately, this isn't something you can take care of for her, unless you travel with her. However, you can call the manager after your boss's stay and compliment the hotel staff that were especially good to your boss and helpful to you. Until you're familiar with your boss's personal habits, you need to ask her what amenities are important to her at a hotel and anticipate what she will need. For example, if your male boss is attending a black-tie event while out of town, you should make sure the hotel has a valet to press his tuxedo, shine his shoes, and possibly help him tie his bow tie. When you make your boss's reservation, check to make sure the services that she or he needs are offered.

Services hotels offer include:

- Valet and laundry services
- Business centers with copiers and computers
- In-room fax machines
- Computer port lines in rooms to hook up to the Internet and check e-mail
- Check-cashing services (if your boss needs money and there isn't an ATM nearby)
- Fitness centers and pools
- Nonsmoking rooms

These are not only reasonable but expected services you should line up for your boss.

Below is an example of a travel schedule for George while he worked at the White House.

SCHEDULE FOR GEORGE STEPHANOPOULOS
TRIP TO CLEVELAND, OHIO
THURSDAY, JULY 3

NB.   The weather in Cleveland is hot, sunny, and dry. It was 92° F. yesterday.

8:30 A.M.   Depart Home
                  Car to pick you up curbside
                  Capitol Car Service: Tel. 202-123-4567

8:50 A.M.   Arrive Reagan National Airport

9:30 A.M.   Wheels Up: Delta Flt. #3456

9:45 A.M.   Wheels Down Cleveland
                  Car to meet you outside baggage claim
                  AAA Car Service: Tel. 216-123-4546

10:30 A.M.   Arrive at the Sheration Marquis Hotel (Tel. 216-123-2000)
                  You will be met curbside by Sam Brown of the Chamber of Commerce

11:00 A.M.   Cleveland Chamber of Commerce Community Service Awards
                  Baroque Room, Banquet Level
                  Introduction by Sam Brown (10 minutes)
                  Keynote Address (20 minutes)
                  Presentation of Awards (10 Minutes)

11:45 A.M.   Photo Op with Award Winners
                  Meet and Greet

12:15 P.M.   Depart Hotel
                  Car to meet you curbside (same driver)

12:30 P.M.   Lunch with John Brown, editor in chief of *Cleveland Daily News*
                  La Fou Frog
                  Tel. 216-567-8989

1:30 P.M.	Depart restaurant en route airport
	Car to meet you curbside (same driver)
1:45 P.M.	Arrive Airport
2:30 P.M.	Wheels Up: Delta Flt. #4567
4:30 P.M.	Wheels Down Washington National Airport
	Car to meet you outside baggage claim
	Capitol Car Service: Tel. 202-123-4567
5:30 P.M.	Arrive White House
6:15 P.M.	Meeting in chief of staff's office

chapter 8

Boxers or Briefs? Keeping Your Boss Informed

Goal: To make your boss as efficient as possible.
Give her the information she needs, quickly and easily.

What Are Briefs and When Should You Write One?

Briefs are informative memos. Different industries call them briefs, briefings, or briefing books—but all these terms are interchangeable for the same thing. You'll have an opportunity to write a briefing memo for your boss if his time or attention is in short supply and you can't meet with him and give him information verbally. Write briefing memos if you need to give him an update on a project you are overseeing, or if you attended a meeting which he missed (page 128). However, the most common type of briefing memo you will prepare for your boss is one which will give him information on meetings and events you have scheduled (page 130). This includes travel briefings which will accompany his schedule for a trip. The most important thing to remember regarding briefings is that you should keep them short and useful.

Before I became George's assistant on the '92 Clinton campaign I spent a couple of weeks helping put together Governor Clinton's daily briefing book. It was an involved collection of briefing memos, each one of which gave him background information about every event on his schedule. Of course, I spent most of my time typing other people's work and photocopying, but one day I was allowed to write a briefing memo to the governor. He was attending an event at a bowling alley (yes, this was early in the campaign), and I found myself instructing the future president of the United States on how to pick out his bowling shoes and put them on. Hopefully a potential leader of the Free World can pick out and put on shoes in a bowling alley without written instruction. I had taken my job of briefing the candidate too literally and didn't have the experience to give him just the information he would actually need. It took me a while to learn this lesson. Much later, in the White House, I was unpacking George's briefcase after a trip and pulled out the briefing book I had carefully put together for him. It was obvious that George hadn't even looked at it beyond a quick glance. Remembering my naïve memo to Governor Clinton, I realized that briefing memos must be written for the reader and reflect what he or she doesn't yet know and really needs to know.

General Briefing Memos

Even if you have a casual interaction with your boss, type up your memo with a certain formality, using the standard form you see on memos in your company. It's good practice for you to learn how to write a memo, and let's face it; you are giving this memo to the person with the most influence over your career.

- State the reason for the memo in the first sentence.
- Use bullet points.
- After you have written the memo, edit it and remove anything that is not crucial.
- Be clear, precise, and brief.

Travel Briefings

I refer to these as "books" out of habit because whenever the president travels a thick book of briefing memos is created. My guess is that your boss will not need as much information as the president when he travels, but you should still supplement his schedule (see page 122) with a brief which can include the following:

- **If your boss is traveling to an unfamiliar city, give him background information on where he's going.** You'll need to use the Internet, to learn as much as you can about your boss's destination. (If your company does not automatically give its employees access to the Web, tell your boss that you need it and get online as soon as possible.)

- **Is there information you can gather from other members of your boss's staff that would help him on his trip,** such as background information on the reason for his trip? For example, if he is going to tour a factory which is a possible new manufacturing site for your company, the person who recommended the factory should have information on the factory's history, productivity, etc.

- **What will the weather be like where he is going?** Does he need sunglasses? Is there a pool where he'll be staying or a nearby golf course? What is the dress code for the different events he'll be attending? (He needs to know all this before he packs for the trip).

- **Are there people he needs to remember that he'll be seeing on this trip?** Or perhaps there are people he might want to call locally if he gets some spare time. Create a list of professional and personal contacts local to where he's going to be and their telephone numbers for him.

- **Are there any local current events about which he needs to be aware,** either out of polite interest, or that will impact his plans?

- **Include lists of useful phone numbers, your boss's schedule, agendas for meetings, speaking notes, etc.**

Put everything into a three-ring binder or whatever format your boss prefers, so that the pages won't be lost, and so that it is easy to read on a plane or in a car. Use the binders which have front and rear pockets because these are useful for airline tickets. Make an identical copy of your boss's travel briefing book and keep it in your bible (see chapter 3) for reference while he's on the road.

* * *

Below are examples of briefing memos that I might have written to George while we were in the White House.

Briefing your boss on a meeting he missed.

TO: George
FR: Heather
RE: WWII Commemorative Events Mtg., 01/27

Friday, 09/01	Division Review and Passing of Ships
Saturday, 09/02	Memorial on Aircraft Carrier
	Keynote Address at Cemetery—12,000 attendees
	Veterans Parade
Sunday, 09/03	Ecumenical Service—75 minutes
	Musical Review Show (a la Bob Hope)

Q. Should the event be international with representatives from different countries invited?

A. NSC: Absolutely not. Sec. Perry will send a letter to the defense ministers of countries involved inviting them to the commemoration but making it clear that it would be inappropriate for Foreign ministers and heads of state to attend. The Japanese and Russians have never signed a peace agreement and which would we invite, China or Taiwan? Requests for exception must be dealt with carefully (GB wants to send royalty). There are domestic policy issues to consider: the postage stamp and the Enola Gay exhibit are examples of the sort of problems that can arise.

General K: They would like to include representatives from other countries, but will respect any decision from the White House.

Q. What leaders should be invited to the Ecumenical Service?

A. A rabbi will be invited. Billy will ask Leon about inviting the Pope. General feeling at the table is that his attendance would be a logistical nightmare and take the focus away from the veterans.

Communications: Evelyn is concerned that POTUS will be overexposed with the above schedule. Would like to see him participate in one, maybe two speaking events per day. Don agrees. NSC suggests that Perry could represent POTUS at some events. The general feels that this would be a poor substitute for presidential involvement. However, the general will present Billy and Evelyn with a prioritized list of the above events.

Briefing your boss with more information.

TO: G
FR: H
RE: The Gap Ad Campaign

GAP's new advertising campaign will be similar to its old one in that it will feature public figures wearing khakis. This time they want to emphasize what they (optimistically) perceive as a movement toward casual dress in the workplace. To this end, the public figures will be successful young career people.

You are the only political figure they have approached. Others who have agreed to participate are the CEO of Starbucks, the editor of WIRED, the owner of Burton Snowboards, and John Bryant. The ads will be seen in a nationwide publications and some billboards (bus stops, etc.).

They are paying a standard $750 fee; however, many of the subjects are contributing the money to charities. They would be happy not to use your title in the identification under your name on the ad, and in fact, wonder if they should instead list you as the supporter of a certain charity or foundation.

You would sit for the portrait with Richard Avedon at the end of March in NYC.

There is no reason you are legally prohibited from doing this, as you would not use your title or accept the fee. However, if you are interested in participating, I will contact the Counsel's Office.

As to whether it makes sense for you to do it, I expect the pain would outweigh the gain.

Below is an example of a briefing memo for an event or meeting, either in town or while traveling.

TO: George
FR: Heather

What:　　　　Labor Event
When:　　　　November 2, 1994–12:30 P.M.
Where:　　　　P.E. Gym at Washington High School, Duluth, MN

PURPOSE:　　　　To meet with labor leaders who are strong Clinton supporters.

BACKGROUND:　　　　The participating labor unions have supported the administration on key legislative issues and provided substantial financial support throughout the last year and a half.

They will be actively involved in GOTV activities from now through the elections and will be helpful to the Democratic ticket in Minnesota.

PARTICIPANTS:　　　　John Brown, president of the CWA, and Sam Smith, president of the SEIU, will attend.

PRESS:　　　　No press.

SEQUENCE OF EVENTS: Meeting followed by photo op.

REMARKS:　　　　None.

Making a List and Checking It Twice: Gifts

Goal: To maximize your boss's ability to focus on his job by remembering dates for him.

Making Your Boss Look Good

An important part of your job is being your boss's memory, and making her appear to be a more considerate person than perhaps she has the time to be. You need a system for remembering dates that are important in your boss's life. The majority of these dates will be birthdays, but there are also anniversaries, graduations, births, and weddings. The act of remembering and acknowledging an important date ranges from sincere, in the case of a loved one, to good public relations, in the case of someone with whom your boss wants to score points.

Gather Important Dates

Gather people's birthdays in the same way you will gather their contact information. Ask for their birthdays when you ask for their phone and fax numbers (see chapter 2) and record the information in your database. Don't ask for the year anyone was born—asking this could be offensive, or illegal if you are talking to someone who works for your boss. In your database there will be space in each field for notes or comments; always take the time to add any personal information that you learn about the person that might later be useful in buying gifts: for example, a spouse's name, a favorite color, or a hobby. Ask your predecessor and your boss if there are birthdays that you need to make note of, and input these into your database. And as always, pay attention; write down dates that are mentioned around you.

Remembering Dates

There are two simple ways to make sure that you don't forget a birthday or anniversary. Your computer will probably have an "alarm" feature which can remind you of upcoming important dates when you turn it on in the morning. (This comes with all personal digital assistants such as Palm Pilot, and with Microsoft Outlook, which is part of the Windows package.) However, I have always preferred the old-fashioned method of putting all birthday and anniversaries on a calendar designated especially for this. At the end of every month and beginning of a new one, I look through the birthday and anniversary calendar and mark dates to remember on my Week-at-a-View desk diary for the entire coming month. Whatever system you decide to use, make sure that your system gives you enough forewarning of an upcoming date to allow you to make arrangements to acknowledge it (to send flowers or a card, or buy a gift).

Who?

There are four categories of people whose birthdays (and other important dates) will need to be remembered:

- Your boss's Significant Other, whether a spouse, a girl-friend, or boyfriend
- Family members (siblings, parents, children, nieces, nephews, godchildren, etc.)
- Professional associates, coworkers, and members of staff (this includes people who work for your boss in her private life, such as babysitters and housekeepers)
- Friends

Some Tips

- **Flowers are always a safe** and easy way to acknowledge a birthday or anniversary. If he's modern and sophisticated, it is okay to send a man flowers.

- **Parents are often more touched if someone remembers their child's birthday than their own.** If you want to impress a coworker or professional contact on behalf of your boss, you'll score a lot of points (for your boss) if you send a gift for his or her child.

- **Don't forget graduation** every year in May. Make notes throughout the year of college and high school students who'll be graduating (again, remember the children of your boss's colleagues), and in April present your boss with the option of sending gifts to them.

- **Do not be surprised if your boss uses company money to buy gifts for people in her personal life.** It is pretty common to take advantage of the company in this way, especially when an executive gets to a certain level on the food chain. However, to protect yourself in case your boss ever gets into trouble for this graft, and until you know your boss's habits very well, always ask her how she wishes to pay for things and get her to tell you if she wants to charge the expense to the company.

- **Don't forget to remind your boss that a gift was sent** in her name and what that gift was so that she can take the credit for it.

The Holiday Season—Update the Database

The holiday season presents a great opportunity for public relations outreach, and a nightmare for an assistant. In anticipation, you need to start organizing and updating your database in September every year (in any case, this needs to be done annually regardless of the holiday season). Look through every name and call to confirm all contact information if you have any doubt that it's not completely current. If you work in a busy office and have a large database, this will be a time for you to legitimately request to hire an intern or a temp because making these calls can be very time-consuming. If you do hire a temp or intern, make sure that you make good use of her time. If you have never had anyone work for you before, this can be a challenge. Get organized before the temporary help arrives. Decide what goals you want to set for her to accomplish, and put together the materials she'll need before she gets to your office. (Nothing is worse than having a temp sitting around waiting for you to give her directions—she'll be paid by the hour no matter if she's working or not). For example, if the temp has been hired to help you update your database, you should print your phone directory and highlight the names you think need to be called before she arrives. Write a script for her. Literally type out exactly what you would like her to say on the telephone to everyone she calls. Remember, the temp will be representing you, your boss, and your company. Make sure you have a work-space set up for her before she arrives. And schedule her arrival for a time when you'll be able to take the time to explain your expectations to her clearly. Make a list of other jobs for her to do should she finish making the update calls earlier than expected. And finally, treat her well. Be respectful. I once had a temp who was a graduate student at Harvard getting her Ph.D. in international relations. Be open to her questions and patient with her confusion. Remember your first day on the job?

Talk to Your Boss

During a weekly meeting with your boss early in October you need to raise the issue of holiday gifts and cards. Ask your boss the following questions:

- **Does she want your help in organizing her holiday gifts and cards?** (If your boss has a spouse, she might want you to organize only the professional gifts and cards.)
- **What (flexible) spending limits does she want to set** for the gifts?
- **Does she want separate cards** sent to her professional and personal lists? If your boss is religious, she might want a card with a religious message for her personal list, and a card with a secular message for her business list. Or her personal card might be produced from a family photo.

- **Does she want a card ordered from a favorite charity?**
- **Most large companies produce a generic card for the company,** and you can request the number you need for your boss from an administrative office. If your company does this, does your boss want to use this card for her professional list (and her personal list)?

Create Lists

Once your database is updated and you have met with your boss and have some direction from him, start producing lists from the database. If you have any doubts about someone, include his or her name on these lists; it can be edited out later. It is harder to remember someone left off a list than to remove a name unnecessarily on a list. You will need five (possibly six) lists and they are as follows:

- **Business associates** (including staff) to receive a gift under a certain amount of money
- **Business associates** (including staff) to receive a gift over a certain amount of money
- **People in your boss's personal life** to receive a gift under a certain amount of money
- **People in your boss's personal life** to receive a gift over a certain amount of money
- **People to receive a holiday card.** (You might have to split this list if your boss wishes to send one card to personal contacts and another to business contacts.)

Get your boss to edit the lists—she'll want to add and remove names and move people from one list to another. The software that you use for keeping your database will have options for printing out lists from the database. There will be a way to mark the fields (names) that you want printed on a certain list.

Gift Ideas

After the names on the lists are complete, start putting gift ideas next to the names on the gift lists. Again, get your boss to edit the gifts. Obviously if your company produces something which is appropriate for gifts, this should be the gift, at least for every professional associate. It's tacky to give coworkers and your boss's staff gifts of company product. Food is an easy and well appreciated gift both for professional and personal contacts. Alcohol is usually appreciated, although there can be sensitivities (the recipient might not drink for moral or health reasons) so make sure you know it will be well received before you send it. Find out the names of companies that produce gift baskets of food and alcohol. You can specify the amount that you want to spend on each basket. Sending the same gift to everyone on your boss's professional gift list isn't a problem. Request catalogues of gift companies (if someone sends something nice to your boss, save the information on the company that sent it) and keep them on file.

The Card

After the card list is complete, present your boss with some card designs and messages for her approval. If you're having cards specially printed, make sure you order them early enough to get them from the printer, and to get them signed and mailed. Ask the printer for a firm date when the cards will be ready, and be realistic about your workload and how quickly your boss will sign the cards. You may have to push your boss not to delay the decision of what card to order. As soon as the card list is approved, you can begin to print out sheets of address labels.

The Last Push

By Thanksgiving, all of the gifts on your lists should be approved, and the holiday cards in your office. In the month between Thanksgiving and Christmas, you'll have to purchase the gifts (and possibly wrap and send them, unless this is being done by the gift company), and get your boss to sign all the cards and mail them out. Schedule time for cards to be signed. You should present them to your boss in small numbers so she isn't overwhelmed. Cards that merely require a signature can be signed while she's on the telephone; however, cards that require a personal message will need her full attention. Put Post-it Notes on cards that require a personal message, reminding her of the message she needs to include.

Be prepared for last-minute additions to both the gift and card lists. If you order cards, or many of a certain gift, order extras. Keep copies of your gift lists and card lists, and a copy of the card for reference in subsequent years so that you don't duplicate it. Also, next year you can work off the lists from last year as a starting point.

chapter 10

The Gatekeeper

**Goal: To maximize your boss's time by stop-
ping people from wasting it.**

There will be people both internally and from outside the company that constantly want time with
your boss, and you'll have to tell many of them
"no." They won't like being told "no," and often
their egos will be hurt. Everyone who comes into
your office, or calls your office requesting time
with your boss, will believe that he has a worthwhile reason to talk to your boss. If you and your
boss don't think his reason is worthwhile, and he's
denied time with your boss, he might see this as a
personal insult. He'll want to blame someone
other than himself and it will be you because you
told him he couldn't see your boss.

Often a woman in the assistant position will
have to deal with being perceived negatively when
she's a gatekeeper and she denies access to her
boss. Firm and businesslike behavior in a man is

139

expected and considered appropriate, but in a woman the same behavior can get her labeled a "bitch" or a "ball breaker." This is unfair, and can be emotionally tough for some women to accept, because most of us want to be liked and understood (not to mention the blatant sexism). But as a good assistant, you may have to be the bad guy, while your boss is allowed to be the good guy. If your boss has been avoiding talking to someone for days, and then he runs into this person by the elevator or in a restaurant, the chances are that your boss will deny ever knowing that the person has been trying to reach him for days. Your boss will tell the person to call you immediately to schedule an appointment, and when the person calls, he or she will probably be condescending to you. Hopefully for your sake, your boss will finally agree to meet with this person, because if he still doesn't, you will have to deal with someone who will become increasingly angrier with you. But never, ever should you make your boss look bad by being honest and telling someone that he isn't interested in talking to him. (The only time this sort of frank honesty would be acceptable is when you are talking to salesmen making unsolicited pitches for your company's business.)

Don't Be Mean

It is depressingly easy to become a bitch in an assistant role. When you're stressed out from working long hours juggling lots of different responsibilities and taking care of a demanding boss, it can be easy to tell people "no" abruptly without really listening to them and trying to be helpful. Demands are constantly being made on an assistant. You'll be pulled in many different directions, and every time the phone rings or a fax comes in, it will represent someone wanting something from you. Also (and this is the ugly side of being an assistant), you can easily become puffed up with self-importance because you have the power to say "no" to someone. However, it is crucial that you do everything possible to avoid this, most importantly because you won't like yourself, but also for your current and future career. Stay humble; remember that your boss is the person of power and influence, not you. And remember that you have been, and will be again, the person on the other end of the phone talking to an assistant and trying to get in to see the boss. If you allow yourself to become someone that you don't like, you'll quickly become bitter in your job and you'll be unhappy, which will be bad for you personally (you'll hate going to work every day) and professionally (your boss and coworkers will stop liking you). What goes around comes around, so don't alienate people. You need to be liked and respected by people at all levels within your company, your industry, and beyond. You'll need good relationships to get things done efficiently or to beg special treatment for your boss when needed. Remember that there is a difference between courting favor and kissing ass, and it comes down to respect and sincerity. If your goal in developing a relationship is mutual respect people will sense it, but they will equally be able to tell if you are sucking up to them for superficial, personal gain. People need to like you to want to do things for you. And while you currently have your boss's proxy and can demand that people do things for you because of his stature, think to the future—one day you may work with the people who you are making demands of as an equal or subordinate.

Judging Your Boss's Mood

The first step in being a competent gatekeeper is knowing what your boss wants. As with all aspects of your job, you'll become much better at this with experience, but initially you'll need to ask your boss for guidance, and learn to read your boss's body language. Pay attention to which people your boss tends to blow off by not returning their calls or avoiding. Are there people that you see wasting your boss's time—for example, someone on his staff who comes in every day to ask him questions that someone else could answer? Ask your boss if he wants you to intercept the employee and help her get the information she needs from someone else. Can you tell if your boss is bored or annoyed? Pay attention to the way he sits and the things he says when he is engaged in a conversation versus when he is trying to end one. Ask him if you can help him by interrupting his calls or meetings when you sense he wants to get away but doesn't want to be rude. Helping your boss like this is a way in which you will become a real partner to him and earn his gratitude and trust.

Who?

People who want time with your boss will come in two categories, from inside the company and from outside. Internally the people will be

- **Your boss's superiors,** who must never be denied access to him
- **His staff,** who will get scheduled time with him, but probably not as often or as soon as they want it, and
- **His coworkers,** who are on his level.

It will be most complicated for you to judge the access his coworkers should have to him, because of office politics. Some will have a legitimate need to see him, and others will not, but will have to be seen because of power and influence. The external requests for your boss's time will be a mixture of people he needs and wants to see and people who want to waste his time.

How?

Requests for time with your boss are going to come by mail, telephone, and in person. The first two are the easiest to deal with because you'll have an opportunity, if you need one, to get direction from your boss. People who drop by to see your boss without an appointment are more difficult to judge, but they'll most likely be from within the company, and as above, his superiors will always get access to him. But peers and staff will be have to be judged on a case-by-case basis: Consider what your boss is doing at that moment and what the visitor wants to discuss.

Excuses

When making excuses for why your boss cannot see someone, you should rarely tell the truth if your boss doesn't want to see him or her. You should use the schedule as an excuse, such as your boss is in a meeting or out of the office. Always be very firm but very polite. Be careful that you don't tell a lie that can be found out; for example, don't lie and tell someone within the company that your boss can't meet with him because he is at an all-day meeting out of the building. What if he runs into the person in the hallway later in the day?

Saving Your Boss

The real skill in being a gatekeeper is ending a meeting or conversation. There are two possible ways you can do this:

Method 1: You could arrange in advance to save your boss if he's going into an obligatory meeting, which he knows he'll want to get out of before it ends. Decide with your boss upon an excuse for you to use to interrupt and call him away from the meeting. You may say he has a telephone call or is needed at another meeting. For maximum believability, throw in some specifics: "I'm so sorry to interrupt, but you're late for your weekly meeting in the chief of staff's office."

Method 2: You haven't discussed rescuing him but your gut tells you that he wants to get out of a meeting. To offer him an escape route (and remember, you may have misjudged and he won't take it) you can stick your head into his office and say, "I'm sorry to interrupt, but Jane just called and says that she needs to speak with you immediately. Can she wait or do you need to return her call now?" This will allow your boss a chance to end the meeting with a gracious excuse, or dismiss you and continue. Make sure you use an excuse that will be clearly false to your boss; don't alarm him by telling him that he has an emergency call from the company's CEO.

In 1993 a nightmare for George came true; two media-hungry graduate students from California started the George Stephanopoulos Fan Club complete with meetings, a newsletter, lapel pins, and a media blitz. While now it seems like nothing more than an excuse for some good-natured ribbing from his friends, at the time it was very bad for George because he was in a constant struggle to control his image. He was perceived by some in Washington, and portrayed by the national media, as too young, too handsome, too smart, and too arrogant. Although everyone in Washington is arrogant and many are smart, youth and beauty are resented in the extreme. A fan club just gave George's critics more ammunition. However, George and I had to walk a tightrope. We had to be nice enough to the fan club organizers not to piss them off and generate more negative media about George being too arrogant to even have time for his own fans, but not to assist them in a way that would open George up to the criticism of actually supporting his own silly fan club. The obvious solution was for me to keep them away from George so that they wouldn't have anything like photos or interviews that would give the impression that George had endorsed the fan club. I was a bitchy gatekeeper, and he was a very busy but nice Very Important Person.

I managed to keep them away from George for a while, but the cofounders were persistent, and George decided to agree to meet them. However, we agreed that I would "save" him after five minutes with them. I had the ultimate excuse, which I tried not to use unless absolutely necessary, "George, the president needs to see you in the Oval Office." People actually liked being left for the president, as it added drama to their experience of meeting George Stephanopoulos in the West Wing of the White House. In a *New York* magazine piece on George's fan club in the February 6, 1995, issue, one of the club's presidents described their meeting with George, and my gatekeeper role: "The seven-minute meeting took place on October 21, 1993 . . . George came out, and the hair was great. We spoke for seven minutes. Suddenly we noticed that Heather Beckel was standing about six feet away with her arms folded. George stood up and we knew our time was over." The downside is that earlier in the piece I was referred to by name as "George's allegedly charmless assistant." Being a good gatekeeper is an important part of being an assistant, and it'll help if you have thick skin and a strong sense of righteousness.

Getting Personal With Your Boss Beyond the Office Walls

Goal: To make your boss more efficient at work by taking care of the personal details of his life.

Different Bosses, Different Needs

The amount to which your boss will want you managing his personal life will differ greatly between individuals and industries. But the chances are you'll be responsible for at least some duties which fall into the category of personal errands. The more senior an executive is the more likely he is to feel entitled to ask you to do personal errands for him as part of your job, even though you are paid by the company. The

146

executive will feel justified in expecting you to manage his personal affairs because anything that makes him more efficient and able to concentrate on his job makes him more valuable to the company. The two most important women in the life of David Wilhelm, the campaign manager for Clinton's '92 presidential bid, were his wife, Degee, and his assistant Martha Swiller. Degee used to joke that she was his night wife and Martha was his day wife. Some executives have two assistants, one in the office and a personal assistant who works out of their home. If this is the case in your situation, you must work closely with your counterpart. You can help each other by coordinating schedules, sharing information, and warning of your boss's mood swings. However, an executive with two assistants is rare, and most likely you'll be expected to play both roles.

Your Ego

It can feel demeaning to run personal errands for a boss; it can make you feel angry too. Your ego can feel bruised and you might feel you are too valuable and smart to be doing such work. But you need to get over these feelings and not waste any time resenting being asked to do personal errands for your boss. Remember this; almost everyone starts their career at the bottom of the ladder doing the work no one else wants to do. You don't have any work experience and you have everything to learn. If making your boss more efficient at his job involves you taking care of his personal errands—then that is what you must do. If you're a guy reading this, be warned: This issue of ego and doing personal errands is why women tend to make better assistants. More women than men don't mind submerging their egos and taking care of someone else on every level. But if you're a woman reading this, also be warned, because your willingness to allow your ego to be submerged and to take care of someone is why it can take longer for you to get promoted than the men at your level. Also, to be blunt, this is part of the job, so you need to decide whether you want the job or not.

Anticipate and Take the Initiative

To combat feelings of worthlessness, stay motivated. Ask questions and use your brain; try to think of ways to do a better job than is expected of you. Personal assistant work is no different than that in the office, in that the work itself is uncomplicated and pretty easy; however, the skill comes in doing it all at the same time, under pressure, and with grace. The fundamentals of being a great personal assistant are the same as those of being a great office assistant. Don't wait for problems to be solved; anticipate them, and pay attention to details.

Emotional Investment

Like in the office, you must know everything about the universe in which you are working, and this, of course, is your boss's personal life. This raises two issues—one of trust and confidentiality, which is covered in chapter 13, and the other of getting emotionally close to your boss. When we become friends with someone, we become intimate with him and learn all the details of his life. You'll learn all the intimate details of your boss's life, take care of him, and probably spend more time with him than you do with any of your own friends or family. However, he isn't your friend and this can get very emotionally confusing, particularly if your boss is someone you admire. It's complicated when your happiness and job satisfaction rely entirely upon someone else's happiness, and the relationship can develop like a one-sided love affair where one partner is doing all the taking and the other all the giving. Assistants are emotionally invested in their bosses; they usually admire them because the boss is what the assistant aspires to be one day. Because of this emotional investment, it's easy to get your feelings hurt by your boss and his treatment of you. You need to protect yourself by maintaining an emotional distance from your boss and from your job as his assistant. No matter how close and friendly you are, at some point your boss will treat you as an employee, and if you have allowed yourself to forget that this is what you are, it can be heartbreaking.

It's almost inevitable for an assistant to have a "crush" on her boss, and while it makes her more vulnerable to hurt feelings, it can actually make the assistant better at her job. I'm talking about a nonsexual crush, the kind of crush that is about admiration and thinking someone is the coolest person in the world. It's the kind of crush kids have on other kids, particularly ones older than themselves. It's easier to live to please someone, and remember all their personal habits, desires, and needs if you have a crush on him. If the gender roles are correct the crush can be romantic in nature, but even a straight guy can have a nonsexual crush on a male boss who he looks up to. And just to make your life really messy, it's also possible that your boyfriend (or girlfriend) will be jealous of your relationship with your boss because of all the attention and time you are required to give to his wants and needs.

George's behavior with President Clinton at the White House teaches the best lesson in maintaining emotional distance with a boss. Clinton likes to be friends with his staff and of course, this was very seductive. After all, not only is he charming and fun to hang around with, he was the president. What could be more flattering than to have the president ask you about your personal life, or invite you to watch a movie in the White House theater? The president and his family watched movies there on Friday nights when he was at home and he would invite various friends and staffers to join them. He often invited George, but George always declined. The president and George spent a lot of time together, and Clinton, who is a curious person, would ask George personal questions, but George always politely deflected the inquiry. George knew he should not get more entangled with his boss than he automatically was because of the nature of his job.

It is possible that you won't like your boss at all and this will make it hard for you to do your job—particularly the personal assistant duties. If you really hate or disdain your boss then you should question why you are working for him. Are you going to be able to enjoy any part of your work and will you learn anything positive from the experience? If you feel that your boss has crossed a line and is asking you to do personal work for him that is inappropriate and makes you uncomfortable, then your only option will be to talk to him and attempt to set boundaries. But be aware of your actual job description and expectations within your industry for an assistant's role. Again, if your boss's behavior is objectionable to you, then you should question why you are working for him. The hard truth is that it is unlikely that a successful executive will change his behavior and expectations to suit his assistant.

Husbands and Wives

If your boss is married, you will need to learn very quickly how to deal with his spouse. This is always true of wives, but almost never true of husbands. Managing your relationship with your boss's wife will be one of your most difficult lessons in diplomacy. Be respectful; she is his life partner. You could be used and caught in the middle of any emotional issues the couple has. Ask your boss politely how he wants you to work with his spouse—use the example of her calling you to check on his schedule. His answer will tell you a great deal about their relationship: He might tell you that you can give his wife any information she requests, or he might tell you to tell her nothing without first checking with him. Unfortunately, often the clichés are true, and the nonworking wives of powerful men can be particularly difficult to deal with; you may find that she's bored, needy, and even jealous of you. If she doesn't have an assistant of her own, she may try to take advantage of you and get you to perform assistant duties for her. Some wives, like assistants, enjoy the reflected glory of their husbands and they don't want to miss out on anything.

This was certainly the case of the wife of a Clinton cabinet member who would routinely call up his assistant and yell at her because the cabinet member would forget to (or intentionally not) tell her about things on his schedule such as dinners, parties, and trips. The dynamic of their relationship was such that she didn't yell at him; the assistant took all the blame for the wife being left out. I know of a very powerful executive in Los Angeles who has a "marriage of convenience" and told his assistant bluntly that he hates his wife. The assistant has to lie to the wife constantly, and goes to great lengths to make sure that she is not included in any of his social engagements. Whatever the situation, make sure that you are clear on what your boss wants.

Stay Organized

Try to schedule the same time every week to do personal errands for your boss. Coordinate it with a weekly meeting your boss has so that he'll be out of the office. This way both you and your boss will know when his personal errands will get done. You'll need to keep well-organized notes on your boss's life as you learn more about it, and mark on your calendar things you need to remember to do on specific dates. Notes on your boss's personal life should be filed and kept with your personal files; obviously the information they contain will be extremely confidential.

The Personal Stuff

The following are the general areas of your boss's life with which you will need to acquaint yourself if you have a boss that expects you to be his assistant outside the office.

- **House(s)**—Keep lists of all the people who service your boss's house(s), such as the housekeeper, pool maintenance person, plumber, electrician, landscaper, etc., with their contact information (get pager numbers in case of emergency) and their schedules for working on your boss's house. Keep notes on the alarm system. Have the address, telephone, and fax numbers written down. Keep written directions to the house(s).

- **Car(s)**—Keep a schedule of when the car(s) needs to be serviced, and the name and contact information of the mechanic. Also keep information on the parking garage, if your boss uses one, AAA membership information, and local tow truck services. Put on your schedule to get the car washed and detailed on the inside.

- **Planes and Boats**—Keep information on where the boat or plane is kept, the name of the pilot or captain, and maintenance information.

- **Family**—Does your boss have children for whom you have

responsibilities? And if your boss has a spouse, work really hard at having a good relationship with her or him. Your boss's spouse can be your best friend or worst enemy.

- **Pets**—Keep information on pets' vets, groomers, dog walkers, and pet sitters.

- **Food**—Does your boss have any dietary restrictions? Keep notes on her likes and dislikes.

- **Medical**—Keep the names of all your boss's doctors and insurance information.

- **Beauty/Health**—Keep information on the spas your boss frequents, names of massage therapists (keep several in case one is not available), hairdressers, etc.

- **Parties**—Keep information on the caterers and florists your boss likes to use for parties. Go ahead and keep information on tent companies, valet services, and any other numbers you come across which could at some point be useful.

- **Financial**—Keep lists of all your boss's bank accounts and their numbers with contacts at the bank. Keep information on his mortgage—the loan number, the amount due, and the address to where the payment should be sent. Also keep all the information on his credit cards. Never, ever forget to mail your boss's bills on time—make a note in pen on your hand if necessary to remind yourself.

- **Club Memberships**—Keep notes on all the clubs your boss belongs to with dates of renewal and costs, including the country club and the gym.

- **Charities**—Keep a record of and information on all the charities your boss contributes to and is interested in.

- **Miscellaneous**—Dry-cleaning, photo developing, shoe repair, etc.

Promote Yourself to a Manager

Goal: To take control without taking over.

Why Be a Manager?

Don't look at your position in the narrow view of an administrative assistant, but rather as your boss's manager. Celebrities have managers who run every aspect of their lives and, to a certain extent, you're doing the same thing for your boss. One of the biggest concerns in promoting an assistant is that she'll be unable to work without constant direction. You can eliminate this concern about you by acting managerial in your role as an assistant. By being a manager of your boss's schedule and office you'll garner more respect from your coworkers, and therefore feel good about your job. Remember your goal: to maximize your boss's time by doing everything for her that you can. You

154

want your boss to focus on the core responsibilities of her job, and leave the rest to you.

How?

Being a manager requires a leadership role rather than passivity. The way to do this is either to take the initiative to solve problems without direction from your boss, or to offer your boss a choice of realistic solutions to problems. A simple example of this would be to decide to refer a caller to your office to someone other than your boss, rather than letting your boss take the time to return the call and refer the individual to someone else.

Here are some tips on becoming a manager within your assistant role:

- **Make it your business to know what's going on.** How do you learn what's going on when you're just a junior employee and an assistant? Ask questions; people enjoy talking about themselves and what they're working on. Pay attention; listen to conversations around you. Educate yourself; read as many of the reports and memos that come into your office as possible and take the initiative to do research on subjects you don't know anything about. Stay informed about the world outside of your office too; read newspapers, stay up on pop culture (entertainment), read the trade publications for your industry, and talk to people. Every industry has its own reference guides; make sure that you have them for your field and that you know how to use them. A word of caution: Never pretend to know more than you do.

- **Understand the goals of your boss and the goals of your company.** Can you answer this question: What is your boss's role at the company? Have a thorough knowledge of the organization. Once you establish yourself as someone with knowledge, people will come to you with questions. At first, this can be as simple as knowing how to request a new piece of office furniture, or the telephone number of a manufacturing plant in another state.

- **Earn the right to be your boss's communicator.** When you understand what is going on and your boss's goals, you'll be able to speak for your boss. For example, someone on your boss's staff will come into the office to ask if he should take the time to expand the report he is preparing for the boss in another area. If you know why your boss requested the report, and what other reports she's assigned to other members of her staff, you can tell the employee if the report should be expanded. Both your boss and everyone who works with her will be grateful that you're able to facilitate another level of communication. However, there will be people who will refuse to talk to you even though you can help them. They'll want to talk only to your boss. If this happens repeatedly with someone you work with consistently, ask your boss to tell the person that he can talk to you if the boss is unavailable. With everyone else, you can just put their messages onto your boss's call sheet with the knowledge that they are shooting themselves in the foot because you could give them the same answer your boss will, only much quicker.

- **Develop impeccable judgment.** All of this instruction I'm giving you builds on itself and you will develop good judgment as you become more educated.

- **Don't allow yourself to become brain dead** and even when you are performing mind-numbing tasks, pay attention to detail. For example, when you are producing form letters in response to correspondence, don't allow yourself to make mistakes because your mind is wandering. Learn to keep your mind focused.

- **Be a team member** and protect your boss from the rest of the staff and vice versa. You can be an invaluable team member in the office by being the liaison between your boss and the rest of her staff. You can help the other members of your boss's staff look good to your boss. I once worked on a campaign where everyone was expected to pitch in and help with all the projects. The campaign manager's assistant had reluctantly agreed to help stuff envelopes with information we were sending out to supporters. She had already helped fill over two thousand envelopes with an invitation to a campaign rally and a map to the location. On this day she was stuffing another one thousand envelopes for an additional last-minute mailing, and the woman in charge of the event stopped by her desk to see how it was going. She quickly realized that the assistant was stuffing the envelopes with the invitation only and she asked: "Where are the maps?" The assistant replied: "No one gave me the maps." She said this in front of the campaign manager. She was letting the campaign manager know that the woman organizing the event had screwed up by forgetting to give her the map, and he panicked and started yelling that the mailing was never going to get out in time, blah, blah, blah. First of all, the assistant who had already stuffed two thousand envelopes with the map and invitation should have alerted the event's organizer that the map was missing, but if she didn't notice, she should have been a team member and protected the other person. She could have said: "The maps are still being copied, I just thought I'd get a head start and get the invitations into the envelopes." And then in private, she should have told the woman organizing the rally that she had never been given the maps.

- **Be helpful,** become the person people go to for solutions to problems.

One time in the White House the chief of staff (COS) came into our office to ask George for a copy of a study that had just come out. Unfortunately, neither George nor I was there and so the COS told the intern sitting at my desk that he was doing some radio interviews in a few minutes and asked did he know where the study was. His response was: "I don't know." That's it. He just sat there and told the chief of staff of the White House: "I don't know." Luckily, another young assistant overheard this exchange and interjected that she would get the COS a copy and bring it to his office right away. She found the study on the Internet, downloaded it, and printed it out for the COS. The lesson is to be helpful, and if you can't actually be helpful, then appear to be helpful. In truth, the intern at my desk had never heard of the study and had no idea how to locate it. But he could have offered to search both my desk and George's desk or he could have offered to contact George or me for the COS. The possibilities for appearing helpful are limitless.

- **Follow up.** If you have a task, make sure that it is completed, beyond the part of the task that is your responsibility. Here is a simple example: A call comes into your office from an associate of your boss. The caller is requesting a favor; his daughter is interested in your industry and would like to apply for a summer internship. You know that even though your boss will want this to happen, she doesn't need to take the call, so you take all the information down and assure the man that someone will contact his daughter. You pass all the information on to the person in charge of setting up summer internships, and you let her know that this request is from someone special. And you make a note to tell your boss that her associate has made the request and you're taking care of it. Basically your job is done; you have competently passed the ball to the next player. However, to take your role as an assistant to the next level you should always follow up: In a few days, call the woman in charge of internships and ask if the request has been taken care of. Continue to call her until it is taken care of. Then call the man who made the request and ask him if everything worked out okay.

- **Don't drop the ball.** If you are the person to whom something has been passed, make sure you take care of it. For example, if you're the person who sets up the summer internships, and you receive the message just described, make sure that you contact the man's daughter as soon as possible.

- **Be reliable and do what you say you'll do.** If you tell someone that you'll take care of getting his daughter a summer internship—make it happen. People don't always do their job. Usually it's not deliberate or laziness, but everyone is busy and some things will get pushed to the "back burner."

- **Do more than is expected.** Don't just get away with doing what is absolutely necessary. If your boss asks for information on a new book that just came out, get her the standard information on the author, publisher, and price, but also go online and print out some reviews and information on the author's former work and biography.

- **Build relationships** with people who can help you make things happen. Cultivate relationships by really listening to people and by being helpful.

- **If you are working on a project and someone steals all the credit,** confront her and let her know that you know what she did. Do it in a joking way so that she doesn't feel too threatened. Make sure that you keep notes on your successes, especially the ones you don't get credit for, because you'll be able to set the record straight when you have a performance review with your boss.

- **Don't take sides in disputes.** Office politics can be warlike; there's often a loser who gets vanquished and you don't want to find yourself on the losing side.

- **Demonstrate that your time is too valuable** to do the crummy work. The only way to do this is by being smart and becoming indispensable. When it's time to do mundane work such as filing or updating the database of contacts, you want to be able to make a case to your boss that it is worth the money to hire a temp to do this work under your supervision, because you are busy working on other projects.

- **Don't make your boss (or anyone else) have to tell you something twice.** Carry your notebook everywhere and write everything down so that you don't forget to do something.

- **Don't take "no" for an answer.** If your boss asks you to do something, and someone else tells you it is not possible, don't go back to your boss and tell her it can't be done because what you are probably telling her is that *you* can't do it. Go after the problem from another direction and ask other people to make it happen if the first person turns you down. Be sure that you have exhausted every option before you go into your boss and tell her what she wants can't be done.

- **Watch your boss's back** and feed her information. Develop your relationship with your boss by helping her out whenever necessary. Let her know if you hear something in the lunchroom that she needs to know.

- **Never say "no" to work.** If someone offers you a role on a project, or asks for your help on one, always do it, no matter if the actual work interests you or not. You will quickly be seen in a positive light as someone to turn to when there is work to be done. Over time you will be offered more interesting work.

- **Imitate the people who have the jobs you want.** Copy the way they dress, their manners, and their speech. And beyond copying their superficial aspects, copy their work ethic. This doesn't mean that you can't be yourself and maintain your individuality, but we all need mentors and people we aspire to be like. Find these people and learn from them.

- **As an assistant you need to think like an executive,** not a "clock puncher." Even though you may not be the highest-level employee as far as personnel is concerned, you can't behave like a drone clerk. You have information and relationships that mean you have to behave like someone at a higher job level, and this can sometimes be tough. An assistant is close to the power and inner circle, but remains on the outside. Through proximity and hours spent together, assistants might feel more comfortable with the senior people in the organization, but they need to remember that at the company picnic they'll hang out with the junior people and other "peons" and there will be events and activities that assistants don't get to attend at all.

Sometimes Taking the Initiative Can Be Risky

After the Democratic convention in 1992, during the presidential campaign, there was a swirl of speculation regarding whom Clinton would choose as his running mate. A team of lawyers and researchers had been assigned to vet the candidates and make a recommendation to Governor Clinton. The campaign was under intense media scrutiny, and the governor and his top staff, including George, were holed up in the governor's mansion waiting for the recommendation to make the final decision. I was alone in the campaign office, very late at night, when the fax came in from the team in Washington stating that Al Gore had no skeletons in his closet, and recommending him as the vice presidential candidate. I tried calling George at the mansion, but he wouldn't take my calls. I paged him, but he didn't call me back. Finally I decided to take the initiative and go to the governor's mansion uninvited with the fax in my hand and break into the inner circle with the news. It turned out to be the right decision for several reasons: George was able to be the one to deliver the recommendation to the governor, they were able to make plans for the next day, and I kept the curious media off the trail because they paid me no mind when

I arrived at the mansion gates. I made a decision without guidance from my boss to do something that in almost every case was inappropriate, but which turned out to be the right thing to do.

How Can You Take the Initiative?

Here are some tangible ways to show that you are more than an assistant who needs constant direction.

- **Do the things your boss hates doing.** If your boss always complains about having to write letters of recommendation, offer to write them for her. You can make her job more pleasurable, and take on some responsibility at the same time.
- **Make your boss's life easier** by clearing out the clutter in her office. Make the offer: "May I get this off your desk and take care of it?"
- **When the same type of document always shows up in her out-box** with the same instructions on it, take the initiative next time to not put a similar document in her in-box at all, but follow the instructions that were on all the other similar documents.
- **Don't whine to your boss** or anyone else. If you're frustrated about something at your company, find a solution and make a recommendation to your boss.
- **Take a chance** and make a decision.
- **Don't pass problems to your boss.** If you can, solve the problem yourself or, if you can't, come up with some possible solutions to offer her when you present the problem.
- **There is usually more than enough work to keep everyone busy** at a company and once your boss trusts you, it's pos-

sible that she'll assign projects to you. But if she doesn't, ask for the responsibility of a specific project. Or if you see that another employee in your department is overloaded, offer to take over some of her responsibilities. (But be realistic: Offer to help out by taking the most unappealing of her responsibilities from her.)

During our first six months at the White House, George was the press secretary and he gave daily press conferences scheduled for noon. I sat in on these press conferences and wrote down all the questions, the name of the reporter who asked them, and George's answers—so we could review them later if necessary. However, I took it upon myself to do something else everyday. Several times during the press conferences, a reporter would ask George a question and his response was: "I'll get back to you on that." Not only did I immediately put these reporters on George's call sheet with their questions but whenever possible I called the person in the administration who could give George the information the reporter wanted and either got the answers for him, or alerted him or her that George would be calling soon and what his question would be. The person made sure that they were around to take George's call and prepared to answer his questions, and George's time wasn't wasted.

Own Your Space

While it will take a while for you to become entirely comfortable in your new office space and that of your boss, it is crucial that you eventually "own" the space and department(s) for which your boss is responsible. Knowing your own industry and educating yourself will increase your sense of ownership and confidence. You'll find that people will sense your owner-ship and confidence and will treat you with respect accord-ingly. This confidence will allow you to:

- Initiate and anticipate, which is what it takes for a compe-tent assistant to move to the next level.
- Be your boss's second set of eyes and ears, and help keep her informed of what is going on.

How?

The way to develop this sense of ownership is to know and be familiar with everything in your office. By this I mean: Know when things happen (garbage collection, mail delivery and pick-up, plants watered, etc.); know what every object in your office is (equipment, books, paper, etc.); be familiar with every-one who works with and for your office, from other employees to the guy who delivers the water for the cooler—know their names and, if possible, their kids' names. If your desk, chair, computer, filing cabinets, etc., aren't located where you want them to be, request that they be moved. Make yourself com-fortable in your workspace.

A friend of mine named Julie who once was a spectacular assis-tant is now the executive director of an international women's health and reproductive rights organization. She walked into her office recently to find a package sitting on her chair. She didn't recognize the sender's name and the tracking number was illegible, so she carried it out to her assistant and asked her about it. The assistant had no idea what it was or who it was from—when it arrived she just put it onto her boss's chair for her to deal with. Because of the nature of their work, the workers at this organization have serious security concerns, and my boss followed procedure and immediately called their security team. The security team quickly interviewed my friend and her assistant and decided that because no one was expecting this package or recognized the name of the sender, precautions had to be taken. They evacuated the entire building, x-rayed the package, and then opened it under special bombproof conditions. It contained some information Julie's assistant had requested by telephone the day before. She asked that it be sent as soon as possible, but didn't remember the name of the organization she had called. This assistant clearly has no ownership over her boss's office space and does not control what goes in and out. Her lack of management, not to mention her inability to connect the package with the call she made the day before, cost the organization time and money and lost her the respect of her boss and coworkers.

I heard about a company retreat at which the employees were discussing how to make their business more efficient and do more with less. The vice president's executive assistant was in a small breakout group with several of the company's managers and their task was to find solutions for making business travel more efficient. They started brainstorming and after a while the assistant suddenly contributed: "If we flew business class instead of first class on just our shorter trips, we could save money on airfares." Her idea was met with total silence from the managers around the conference table. Her face turned bright red as someone explained that everyone at the table was required to travel coach with at least fourteen-day advance bookings. The hapless assistant had no idea that her boss was the only person in their division who traveled everywhere first class. When I heard this story, I felt bad for the assistant because I know she must have been excited to be included in the retreat and allowed to leave her desk for the day. I also know that the young woman must have really screwed up her courage to share her idea for cutting costs on airfares at a table of the company's top managers. However, she obviously wasn't doing all she should have to either educate herself or know her universe, and unfortunately, she messed up her opportunity to shine in front of her coworkers.

chapter 13

Discretion and Invisibility: The Perks of Being a Wallflower

Goal: To earn your boss's trust so that you can do a better job as his assistant and learn more.

Don't Gossip!

Never, ever discuss what goes on in your office or in your boss's personal life with anyone. You'll gain your boss's trust and respect when you demonstrate that you can keep your mouth shut. Do not brag by gossiping. Giving away information to show off that you are "in the loop" is an easy trap to fall into, but the momentary benefits of feeling like a big shot aren't worth the cost of losing your boss's trust. If you need another reason for not sharing confidential information, don't do it because it can be against the law. The SEC regulates the passing of information in the corporate world of public companies. Information can be sexy, and you can't trust even your closest friends not to repeat great gossip that you tell them; in fact, it's not fair to expect them not to. If you don't want something spread around, then don't spread it yourself. If you really need to share something, then tell someone who the information means nothing to except as it pertains to you. For example, if you know that your boss is being promoted and this means someone else is going to be fired, and you really want to tell someone, call your mother out-of-state and tell her. She'll be excited for you and the promotion you'll get along with your boss, but she won't repeat the information to anyone that will spread the news around. If you give away information, you'll be found out. Not only will you be embarrassed, but also you'll never be trusted with confidential information again, and you'll find that doors are closed and you're asked to leave rooms. However, once you prove you can keep a confidence, you'll know everything because people will both talk in your presence and confide in you. You'll know a lot of information because of where you sit and the things you see and hear, and you have the power to do a lot of damage. In the White House people are constantly leaking confidential information to the press, and the people who do this have both personal and political reasons. One of the most internally damaging things ever leaked to the press was a list of the salaries of everyone working in the White House. In November 1993 the *Washington Post* printed out all the names, titles, and how much money we made. Everyone became angry and jealous of their coworkers. You'll most likely know how much everyone on your boss's staff earns; imagine if you let one employee know what another made?

* * *

A cautionary tale on the importance of discretion involves James Carville and dates from my days at the White House. For a few months while I was working there I shared an apartment with David Gergen's assistant, Dianna. Gergen was one of President Clinton's senior advisors, who was controversial because he is a Republican. It was a weird scenario as Gergen and George were often at odds within the West Wing, but Dianna and I were friends and had empathy for each other's roles. Dianna and I never had a single problem involving a lack of discretion between the two of us. But one Sunday Dianna and I had a brunch at our home. One of the guests was a reporter from *Time* magazine. During the brunch, a friend of mine (who was also George's girlfriend at the time) came by the apartment. We excused ourselves and went into another room of the small apartment to catch up, leaving Dianna and the others in the dining room. George and his girlfriend had been hanging out with James Carville and Mary Matalin and we gossiped about James and Mary's relationship. Perhaps the reporter went to the bathroom and overheard us, or maybe we were talking too loudly, but two days later *People* magazine came out and the gossip pages contained my conversation with George's girlfriend word for word. (*Time* and *People* have the same parent company, and it is not unusual for reporters to give one another information as favors.) George was furious, and I was humiliated and angry with everyone involved, but mostly with myself. I learned two equally important and painful lessons. I have never fully trusted a journalist since then no matter how much they might be a friend. And even now, I pay very, very careful attention to what I say, where I say it, and to whom. I am constantly aware of how what I say out loud could be used by whomever I am talking to or anyone who overhears me. Also be aware that unless you're talking to your closest family members and best friends, you don't know the connections and allegiances of the person you are talking to. It's never a bad decision to keep silent.

Learning to Be Invisible

As well as earning people's trust, you should acquire a quality of invisibility: allowing people to forget that you're in the room. The way to do this is to be completely quiet, and pretend that you aren't paying any attention to conversations held right in front of you. Trust me, when combined with true discretion, this actually works. Listening to your boss's confidential conversations is not a bad thing, as long as he knows you are listening. Being well informed will benefit both you and your boss. A well-informed assistant is more valuable to her boss, because you can make better decisions and be more helpful. And you'll learn more and have more fun by witnessing your boss's inner circle.

During the general election in 1992 I shared a big office with George, and every morning about 6 A.M. before anyone else arrived at campaign headquarters, James Carville would come into our office. He and George would discuss the confidential, overnight polling numbers, Governor Clinton's mood, and the schedule for the day. Based on this information, they would decide the day's strategy. They knew what they wanted the lead story on the evening news to be, and they tried to shape the governor's activities and predict President's Bush's reaction accordingly. After their plan was set, they went on with their day and set the plan into action. James always returned to our office to watch the evening news and George flipped through the major networks. He and James cheered or cursed based on how closely the stories resembled their goal from the morning. During these morning strategy sessions I never spoke unless spoken to; I sat quiet as a mouse with eyes as big as saucers. And they let me in on (almost) everything: I placed calls to Governor Clinton who was on the campaign trail for them, and then sat there and listened as they talked to him on speaker phone. I set up conference calls with the campaign's consultants (polling, media, and strategy) for George and listened in. What I learned was immeasurable: I learned how George and James negotiated or manipulated to get what they wanted. I learned how they managed a boss with a big personality and ego. And I watched how disciplined they were in everything they did, from the amount of information they gave out to the goals they set for themselves each day.

chapter 14

Negotiating a Promotion

Goal: To take care of yourself, while never letting your boss stumble.

While you learned a lot of important things at college, how to succeed at a job wasn't one of them. You're learning the practical stuff about actually working on the job now. As an assistant you're in close proximity to the people you aspire to be and you're learning how they do their jobs by watching them. You're learning from them everything from the esoteric (how to behave) to the practical (how to conduct a meeting). And you're learning by doing: answering the phone and solving a problem for a caller, scheduling a complicated trip to Hong Kong, etc. You're learning a lot being an assistant. You're learning practical skills which will become the foundation for every other job you'll ever have. And you are learning what direction you want to take in your career. Chances are that when you got out of college you had no idea, or only the vaguest idea, of what you wanted to do with your life. But now that you're working you've had a chance to see a variety of career possibilities in action and you probably have a much clearer idea of what you want to do. You can probably look around your company and your industry and point to people who have jobs you want, and now you know that there is a career path to get there.

If you have implemented the strategies in this book, you're a great assistant. As both a former assistant and boss, I can guarantee that. You've taken the time to educate yourself and train yourself. But you're ambitious and you want more: money, challenges, and responsibilities, and a bigger title. That's great and you should feel encouraged because you're on the right track to get whatever you want.

Promote Yourself

You solve problems every day as you manage your boss's life. Use all the management and problem-solving skills you've learned to work on your own career. You've spent the last couple of years developing a great partnership with your boss. Work with him to make your current position grow as your abilities grow (and hopefully, his job grows too). There's a phenomenon my friends and I used to call "when the assistant needs an assistant." Over time, as you become more and more competent, you'll take on more and more responsibility. Hopefully, your boss's responsibilities will also grow, and at some point you might realize that you don't have time to do a lot of the clerical and admin work of your job. At this point in their careers, several of my friends were able to convince their bosses, who had become increasingly dependent upon them, to hire an additional assistant. They became the bosses of the new hires, and their titles became something like "special projects coordinator." These assistants promoted themselves. Bob Rubin, the former secretary of the treasury, had two assistants, one that did all his clerical work and another, more experienced, who did all the more substantive work.

When you're ready to talk to your boss about formalizing your growing position with another hire, more money, and a better title, choose your time to approach him carefully. You'll schedule your own meeting with him, so don't shoot yourself in the foot: Pick a time he'll be in a good mood. By now you know all his moods and the best way to get his attention and win him over. Use everything you have learned. After all, the point you're going to make to him is that your knowledge of him and your set of skills make you an indispensable employee and worth more money to him and therefore the company. Lay out your argument very clearly; be prepared to list your specific accomplishments and remind him of how well you take care of him, which allows him to do a better job. And be prepared to ask for specific things; as always, offer your boss a solution when you present him with a problem. And be prepared to negotiate with your boss. He may need some time to consider what you're presenting to him or he may only be able to offer you part of what you're requesting.

Have realistic expectations: The chances for promotion and how long it will take to be promoted will vary from boss to boss, and in many industries there is a standard. Some industries, such as the entertainment industry, have very specific and even rigid corporate "ladders" that assistants must climb. For example, at artists' agencies in Hollywood everyone starts in the infamous mailroom and works their way up and out from there. The goal is to become an assistant to an agent and be her apprentice. The way to have realistic expectations is to educate yourself. If possible, talk to the person who had your job before you, and talk to other people within your department and company. Ask about their personal experiences. Talk to your boss and ask him about your chances for promotion. The best way to broach this is to choose an appropriate time, either a very formal time such as your performance review or a very casual time such as at the end of the day in his office when you are both relaxed. Make sure that you are not asking him at a time when you are overly emotional because you are angry or resentful about your job. Simply say that you have been thinking about your future and your career and that you would like his advice. Where does he see you in the next year or two? Remember that luck and your hard work will affect your opportunity for promotion, but again, there are also factors beyond your control, such as your boss and your industry.

Meritocracy

You've been in your job for a while now and you know that what I told you in the introduction is true: There are a lot of crummy workers out there. Workers who do the least amount of work necessary to get by and who aren't smart. Without knowing your company, I feel confident that the chances are good that if you are smart and work hard you'll get promoted. If you're a value to your organization, the organization will want to keep you. If you shine in comparison to your coworkers because you're great at your job and you continually seek out new challenges and responsibilities, people will notice. And the people in a position to promote you will either come up with the idea themselves or they'll be receptive to the idea when you suggest it to them.

Is It Time for You to Leave Your Job?

How do you know when it is time for you to move on from your current job? Ask yourself the following questions, and if the answer is "yes" to any of them, then you are probably ready to move on.

- **Can you honestly say that you have paid your dues at the bottom of the food chain?** Have you learned everything you can in your current job?
- **Are you physically exhausted and feeling bitter about your job?**
- **Are you bored?**
- **Have you tried to fix your current job by getting a better title, more money, or added responsibilities?**
- **Do you know what job you want next and are you qualified for it?**
- **Have you considered that "the grass is always greener . . ."?** I'm not suggesting that you aren't ready to leave your job, and that there isn't something more challenging out there waiting for you. But unless you hate your current job, make sure that you are leaving for something that is truly better than where you are now.
- **Is your boss abusive?**

Telling Your Boss You're Leaving

Telling your boss you want to leave can be bad (unless you were an awful assistant and he's relieved to see you go) because no matter how well you handle it, your departure will result in his discomfort. Unfortunately, it's against his selfish interests to promote you or to help you to leave. Be aware and sympathetic of how unpleasant your leaving will be for your boss. Don't get lazy about your job once you tell him you're leaving, work even harder and be even smarter—make sure your boss is telling everyone how much he'll miss you. Once you have made it clear that you are leaving and he gets over the initial disappointment, he'll help you. Get him on board with your job search by flattering him: Tell him why you're leaving, ask for his help, and tell him that you'll always be indebted to him. Assure him that you'll make the transition go smoothly and offer to interview for your replacement, and of course, train her. Let your boss know that you'll always be available to help him, particularly if you are remaining in the same company or industry. (If you tell your boss that you're leaving, you have to mean it. Out of self-interest he'll probably immediately begin thinking of you as gone and planning your replacement.)

Your announcement that you're leaving should not come as a complete surprise to your boss. Your boss should know what your aspirations are from your performance reviews which give you a chance to discuss your long-term career goals. And once you start to want more challenges and responsibilities in your current job, you should be asking for them as discussed in chapter 12. When you have reached a certain level of competency in your job, you should be working with your boss to make it more satisfactory for you and more productive for him. If you decide that you want to leave your current job either because you don't think there is any possibility for growth or because you have found another more interesting job, discuss your decision respectfully with your boss. If he asks you to "hang in there for a little while longer" and promises that he'll finally make some of the changes you've been requesting, ask for a time line.

* * *

You should have a sense of your boss's expectations for how long you'll stay as his assistant. Usually in a job interview there's a time when you will be asked your career goals, and while you need to make it clear that really you want the job as his assistant, it's appropriate to tell your prospective boss that you'll want to move on to something else after an appropriate length of time (a couple of years is normal). Unless he is completely out of touch with reality, he won't expect you to be his assistant indefinitely. Try to diplomatically find out what his expectations are for how long you'll remain an assistant and if there is a career path at the company to get you promoted. If you don't know what your boss's expectations are, you need to find out by asking at one of your review meetings. I have heard of bosses that have negotiated a time frame for an assistant staying their assistant, and guaranteed a promotion at an initial job interview. But these were rare circumstances: In one case the boss was a jerk and he knew it, so he basically bribed assistants to work for him and stick it out. In the other case, the assistant was highly experienced and didn't want another position as an assistant, so the boss, who really wanted her to work for him, promised her a promotion in a year at their first interview.

In an extreme situation in which you work for a boss who is a nightmare, perhaps you will have to sneak around him to interview for another job. You'll only be able to tell him you are leaving when you give your two weeks' notice. But you should only do this if your boss's temperament leaves you no alternative because it will be almost impossible to hide the fact that you're looking for another job from your boss. If you are trying to keep your job search a secret, be careful who you talk to, and ask people that you meet with to keep your interview confidential since your boss doesn't know you are interviewing. But be realistic; people will tell him that you're looking for a job and you might as well assume that he'll find out.

I didn't manage my departure from the White House well. I stayed too long, and when I decided to leave I just got out as fast as possible. Looking back on it, I can only say that I was physically exhausted and emotionally burned out from being a great assistant, and couldn't think my departure through. Although George knew I was unhappy, and I had been talking to him for several months about either leaving the White House or finding another job within the administration, he was surprised when I actually gave my notice. He was annoyed too because it was a totally selfish decision on my part to leave. Unlike the corporate world, there are obvious beginnings and endings in politics with campaigns and terms, and my leaving halfway through the first term was like leaving in the middle of a major project. The corporate equivalent might be a leaving a boss during an IPO (initial public offering). I gave him a month's notice and, of course, trained my successor (who had been working as George's second assistant for several months already), but still George didn't speak to me for a week after I told him I was leaving. But after the initial shock wore off, George was extremely gracious and has remained a very good friend. You must do a better job in your departure than I did in mine. Plan ahead. If possible, be honest about looking for another job and give your boss plenty of time to get used to the idea of replacing you. Don't let your ego get in the way of helping your boss through the transition; your goal must be to make yourself obsolete and this can be hard on your ego. But believe me, the benefits both personally and professionally of leaving your job in an honorable way far, far exceed any immediate emotional needs you have.

Leaving Is Never Easy

Much as your leaving will be tough for your boss, it'll be tough for you too. In chapter 11 I compared the assistant/boss relationship to a one-sided love affair. Well, you can experience some of the same emotional pangs when you leave your job as you would feel at the end of a romantic relationship. Leaving will probably be an emotional roller coaster for you because while you'll be excited to be going to a new challenge, you might also experience some fear. The chances are that if your next job isn't as another assistant, it will be as a very junior employee of a department and you'll suddenly no longer have the benefits of your former boss's rank and title. You could feel a loss of identity, and loss of the reflected importance that you felt working for a powerful man or woman. For three and a half years I was "Heather Beckel, George Stephanopoulos's assistant," and that afforded me a certain respect and a lot of attention. The important thing to remember is that the respect and attention had nothing to do with my name in that phrase, and everything to do with George's name. When I left the White House, I was just "Heather Beckel" again, and I had to learn to feel okay about that. I can tell you honestly that leaving the White House, and my job as George's assistant, was one of the hardest things I've ever done. If you're having any of these confusing feelings, just remember that you've learned everything you can as an assistant and you no longer want to be one. You have to go out on your own and accomplish something that reflects solely on you. One day you will achieve the level of prestige of your old boss, but if you want to get there as *the* boss then you have to take what may initially feel like several steps down.

Proof That Being an Assistant Can Be a
Great First Job

Nina Plank's first job was as the assistant to a member of
Congress. She now lives in London and recently published her
first book after starting London's first-ever farmers' market.
Nina left Washington and took a job as a copy editor for *Time*
magazine in Brussels. She got her first byline there and was
quickly promoted to reporter. She transferred to London with
Time magazine and after a couple of years was recruited to be
the head speechwriter for the ambassador to the Court of St.
James (the American Embassy in England). Nina grew up on a
Virginia farm, and was surprised and frustrated by the lack of
markets selling fresh produce in London. So she took the initiative and used her immense organizational and managerial skills
to start the farmers' market. She started a cultural revolution in
one of the oldest cities in the world and within three months of
her first market opening, she opened two more in London. A
year and half after the first one opened there are 250 farmers'
markets across Britain. Nina quit her job as a speechwriter and
focuses her time on running the markets. She has also just published her first book, *The Farmers' Market Cookbook,* and is producing a television series of the same name.

I've mentioned Martha Swiller several times in this book.
Martha was my first friend and mentor on the '92 Clinton for
President campaign. She had been working in Washington,
D.C., when she decided to take a huge chance and move to Little
Rock, Arkansas, to be the campaign manager's assistant. Martha
has always had the poise of someone beyond her years; she
earned the respect of everyone on the campaign and became
indispensable to campaign manager David Wilhelm. She was so
indispensable, in fact, that after the election when David

became the chairman of the Democratic National Committee, it was quickly realized that as brilliant and charismatic as David was, he couldn't function without Martha. The power people at the DNC begged Martha to come to work there and let her design her own job description and title and name her salary. She eventually left David and the DNC to be the chief of staff of the Department of Agriculture, one of the largest of the government agencies, with over 300,000 employees. Now Martha is the executive director of California's Planned Parenthood.

Emily Lenzner worked for George and me at the White House as a second assistant. After working for us, she went on to work as the associate producer of a local news program in Seattle. From there she went to Los Angeles where she was the creative assistant for Diane Keaton's production company. After Hollywood, Emily returned to the East Coast and went to work for the president of a major P.R. firm with clients like America Online. She designed her job as a vice president of the firm and acted as the president's deputy, coordinating the projects of everyone on his staff and managing his time. Now Emily is the director of public relations for Active Buddy, the leading instant messaging service worldwide.

How Do You Find a New Job?

If you want to leave your current job there are two possibilities:

- **You don't want to be an assistant anymore, and you want to be promoted to a new job.** If this is the case, you need to identify the job that you want.
- **Or you have discovered that you love being an assistant and want to continue being one, but for a new boss.** If this

is the case, the really good news is you'll have no trouble finding another job because there are always positions available for competent assistants, and you have experience. In fact, you can expect to be promoted at your next job as an executive assistant. This means at your next job you will make more money and work for a more powerful person.

Whether you want to remain an assistant, but for someone other than your current boss, or if you no longer want to be an assistant, there are two options for you:

- **To find another job within your company**
- **Or to go to another company**

Finding a Job Within Your Company

Some companies are great about promoting from within; they believe that the people already on their staff know the company and have a head start on learning a new job. Other companies have low self-esteem and think people are more valuable if they come from outside the company. After working at your company for a while you should be able to tell which kind of company yours is and therefore know what your chances are of getting promoted. As I told you in the introduction, there are a lot of crummy workers out there, and if you work at a company that promotes from within and you show an innate ability to learn, the chances are you will be pegged for a promotion. There are several ways to find another job within your current company:

- **Learn someone else's job** on your own time by asking them to teach you what they do and offering them help in exchange.
- **When you hear that someone is leaving, ask for his or her job.**

- **Use the human resources department.**
- **Watch the job board,** but don't go through the human resources department as they tell you to, go straight to the head of the department that's hiring.
- **Pay attention to the other departments that you are interested in** and learn when they are hiring more people or moving people.

Finding a Job at Another Company

If you want to leave your company and you're starting to search for a job:

- **Talk to your coworkers and ask for their advice,** but only if you have already told your boss you are looking for another job.
- **Methodically go through the database of contacts** for your office and make a list of people who might help you, and call them (again, only do this if you have already told your boss you are looking for another job).
- **Call people with whom you have maintained relationships who have left your company.**
- **Use a headhunter.** I actually don't know anyone who has ever found a job through a headhunter, although I know plenty of people who have registered with them (including me). But I figure they must find jobs for somebody or there wouldn't be so many of them in business.

Being the Boss

Congratulations! You are no longer someone's assistant or you're on your way to being a professional executive assistant. If you've chosen the former path, before too long you'll have your own assistant working for you. Before you get caught up in your new position and forget what it was like being an assistant, think about the kind of boss you want to be. Remember the things your boss did that made you feel great and remember the things you wish he'd done. Emulate the best and use the rest as a lesson in how not to behave. You now know the simple things that can make a world of difference; say good morning and good-bye every day, introduce your assistant, ask your assistant for his opinions, let him know that it is okay to ask questions, and include him in as much of your work as possible. Learning to be a good manager is a bumpier ride than learning to be a good assistant, and you'll probably make some mistakes—but don't let one of them be that you treated somebody badly just because you could. Remember what a great and valuable experience you had as an assistant and pass that on to somebody else.

The Final Truth
About Your Career

When I started writing this book it was out of frustration at the lack of professionalism and ability that I saw in the assistants who came to work for me and for my friends. I selfishly wanted to teach what I know about being a kickass assistant to any assistant willing to learn. But as I started to write the book, I realized that I have something not so selfish to say to assistants and future assistants, and it is that being an assistant really can be a valuable and great experience.

Being George Stephanopoulos's assistant was the coolest job I've ever had. He's a great guy to be around and I got to work in incredible surroundings—but the actual job was also cool. Everything I learned as an assistant I still use today. After leaving the White House I went to Austin, Texas, and helped run the campaign for the reelection of Bill Clinton in 1996. I organized hundreds of field offices in every county in Texas and scheduled hundreds of political rallies and meetings. I was doing exactly what I'd done for George but I was doing it for an entire campaign, and instead of executive assistant my title was executive director.

You really can do anything you want with your own career. All you need is determination and a willingness to work really hard. That's the truth and it has been my experience. After the campaign in Texas, I was recruited to work for Polo Ralph Lauren in New York. I spent two and half years there as the director of corporate communications and got to be involved in the company going public and the global expansion of Polo products and licensees. I got to use my political connections when I brokered a deal between Polo, the Smithsonian Institution, and the White House for Ralph Lauren to donate the money necessary to restore the Star Spangled Banner. I left Polo and I bought my own business, a restaurant in a small town, and that experience has been like earning an MBA. The scale is infinitely less grand than Polo or the White House but the success or failure of the restaurant is totally mine. And now I've written this book. Every career decision I've made has been based on the desire to do something interesting and to have no regrets. It's that simple. I have always had an open mind about trying something new and I've worked really hard at everything I've done.

I hope this book can jump-start your career. I hope it can get you excited to go to work in the morning, learn everything you can, and take advantage of every opportunity. I hope it can make you believe that you can decide what you want to do and take a risk and go out and do it—because you can.

This appendix is written to assist you in planning a trip for a boss to a city with which you are unfamiliar. For each city I've given you an overview to orient you, which will be helpful as you schedule activities for your boss. If your boss is traveling to a city with which you are unfamiliar, read about it here, and then get on the Internet and look at a map. After you've done that, you'll probably have enough information to schedule the trip with no problems, but if you still need to ask questions, at least you'll be asking informed ones. I've also included information on transportation and hotels (all hotels listed have room service, a fitness center, laundry services, and a concierge, unless otherwise noted). Remember that the people who your boss is traveling to meet are a valuable source of local information.

New York City

Overview
New York City is made up of five boroughs: Manhattan, the Bronx, Brooklyn, Queens, and Staten Island. Manhattan is what you think of when you think of New York City, and most assuredly the part of New York City your boss

will be visiting, so I will limit this description to Manhattan alone. The streets of New York are built on a grid: Avenues run north and south, and numbered streets run east and west. Central Park starts at 59th Street and runs north into the streets numbered in the 100s; however there are streets that run through the park so that you can get back and forth from the east to the west sides. There are lots and lots of neighborhoods within Manhattan, and people refer to them when giving directions. Harlem starts in the streets numbered in the high 90s and runs into the 100s, but it is unlikely your boss will travel there for business (unless he's visiting Bill Clinton!). There are the Upper East Side and the Upper West Side—these areas are on either side of Central Park and start in the streets numbered in the high 50s. Midtown refers generally to all the streets from the 20s to the 50s and is most likely where they'll be doing business. Lower Manhattan gets complicated because the grid breaks down, but basically there is the East Village, the West Village, and Soho. Below Soho there is Wall Street and the Financial District. New York is very crowded and the streets are busy all the time; it takes an unusually long time to get anywhere or do anything, which is very stress-inducing, so you must schedule your boss with this in mind.

Airports
There are two airports serving New York. Neither is in Manhattan; both are in other boroughs.

- JFK serves mostly international flights and those from the West Coast. It's only fifteen miles from downtown Manhattan but it takes an hour by car to get to midtown Manhattan.

- LaGuardia is twenty-five minutes by car from midtown Manhattan and serves most domestic destinations.
- Newark airport in New Jersey is also used as an airport to New York City, but usually only when you are trying to save money, because getting into and out of Manhattan to Newark is a pain. It takes forty-five minutes to get from midtown Manhattan to Newark by car.

Hotels—Downtown

Soho Grand Hotel (cool and hip)
310 West Broadway
Tel. 212-965-3000

Mercer Hotel (cool and hip)
99 Prince Street
Tel. 212-966-6060
No fitness facility

Hotels—Midtown

Inter-Continental Hotel
111 East 48th Street
Tel. 212-755-5900

The Drake Swissotel New York
440 Park Avenue
Tel. 212-421-0900

The Waldorf-Astoria
301 Park Avenue
Tel. 212-355-3000

The Essex House
160 Central Park South
Tel. 212-247-0300

Four Seasons Hotel
57 East 57th Street
Tel. 212-758-5700

Grand Hyatt New York
Park Avenue at Grand Central
Tel. 212-883-1234

Le Parker Meridien
118 West 57th Street
Tel. 212-245-5000

Royalton Hotel (cool and hip)
44 West 44th Street
Tel. 212-869-4400

The St. Regis (built in 1904, Beaux Arts décor)
2 East 55th Street
Tel. 212-753-4500

The Paramount (cool and hip)
235 West 46th Street
Tel. 212-764-5501

Hilton New York and Towers
1335 Avenue of the Americas
Tel. 212-586-7000

Hotels—Central Park

The Plaza
Fifth Avenue at Central Park South
Tel. 212-759-3000

Central Park Inter-Continental
112 Central Park South
Tel. 212-757-1900

The Pierre (owned by the Four Seasons Hotels)
2 East 61st Street
Tel. 212-838-8000

Sherry-Netherland Hotel
781 5th Avenue
Tel. 212-355-2800
No fitness facility

Trump International Hotel and Tower
1 Central Park West
Tel. 212-299-1000

Hotels—Uptown

Helmsley Carlton House
680 Madison Avenue
Tel. 212-838-3000
No fitness facility

The Stanhope
995 Fifth Avenue
Tel. 212-288-5800

The Regency
540 Park Avenue
Tel. 212-759-4100

Ground Transport

Taxis are easier to hail on the streets of Manhattan than in any
other city in America, but it can be time-consuming and frustrating looking for one, especially if you are on a schedule. If
your boss travels to another borough, the chances are she will
not find a taxi on the street. One other tip about taxis in

Manhattan: They are almost impossible to find at 4:00 P.M.
because the drivers are changing shifts. If your boss is moving
from one appointment to another at this time, you should
make arrangements with a car service.

Car Services: Empire 800-451-5466
                 Apple 212-265-5255
                 Lincoln Town Car 212-253-2288
                 Town Car 212-873-4477

Los Angeles

Overview
Los Angeles is America's second largest city; the metropolitan
area covers thousands of square miles and contains millions of
people. Greater L.A. is made up of eighty-eight cities. Because
it sprawls across such a vast area, the neighborhoods of Los
Angeles are hard to explain, but here is a simplistic overview.
There is the Downtown, Hollywood (which is sleazy and not
where your boss will be going), the Westside (which is comprised of Beverly Hills, West Hollywood, Bel Air, Westwood
Village–UCLA, Brentwood, Century City, and Culver City),
Santa Monica, and Venice. The San Fernando Valley is not part
of metropolitan Los Angeles, but is one of the areas in the
Greater Los Angeles region and you need to be familiar with it
because the entertainment industry is there.

Airports
LAX is seventeen miles from downtown Los Angeles, and it
takes twenty to thirty minutes to get there by car. The traffic is
legendary.

Hotels—Westside

The St. Regis
2055 Avenue of the Stars, L.A.
Tel. 310-277-6111
Pool

Le Meridien at Beverly Hills
465 South La Cienega Blvd., L.A.
Tel. 310-247-0400
Pool

Park Hyatt Los Angeles at Century City
2151 Avenue of the Stars, L.A.
Tel. 310-277-1234
Pool

Sofitel Los Angeles
8555 Beverly Blvd., L.A.
Tel. 310-278-5444
Pool. No laundry service

Mondrian Hotel
8440 Sunset Blvd., West Hollywood
Tel. 323-650-8999

Regent Beverly Wilshire
9500 Wilshire Blvd., Beverly Hills
Tel. 310-275-5200
Pool

Four Seasons Hotel
300 South Doherny Drive, Beverly Hills
Tel. 310-273-2222
Pool

Hotels—Downtown

Inter-Continental Los Angeles
251 South Olive Street
Tel. 213-617-3300
Pool. No concierge

Wilshire Grand
930 Wilshire Blvd., L.A.
Tel. 213-688-7777
Pool

Hyatt Regency at Macy's Plaza
711 South Hope Street
Tel. 213-683-1234

Ground Transport
There are taxis to hail on the streets in downtown L.A. and on the Westside (Wilshire and Westwoods areas). However, getting your boss a car service will save him a lot of headaches. Driving in L.A. is enjoyable, and parking is easy, but traffic is a big problem and can cause huge delays.

Car Services: Moonlight 310-780-6087
                 Miracle Mile 800-713-5466
                 Limo Connection 800-266-5466

San Francisco

Overview
Union Square is the geographic center of San Francisco. The neighborhoods of Chinatown, North Beach (Little Italy), Downtown (the financial district and the Civic Center), Nob Hill (wealthy residential and hotel area), and SoMa (meaning South of Market, where the Internet companies are located) are

in the Northeast corner. The Northwest corner contains the Presidio, the Golden Gate Bridge Park, and Haight Ashbury. The Castro and the Mission District (Hispanic) are on the east side. Even though San Francisco is on the West Coast, it is very far north, and your boss will need to dress warmly, in layers, all year long. It is a small city, just seven miles by seven miles, but with a population of 750,000.

Airports
San Francisco International Airport (SFO) is fifteen miles south of the city. It takes twenty minutes to get downtown by car.

Hotels—Downtown

Fairmount Hotel and Tower (built in 1906, Victorian décor)
950 Mason Street
Tel. 415-772-5000

Hyatt Regency
5 Embarcadero Center
Tel. 415-788-1234

The Ritz-Carlton
600 Stockton Street
Tel. 415-296-7465
Pool

Triton Hotel (cool and hip)
342 Grant Avenue
Tel. 415-394-0500
No room service

Grand Hyatt Union Square
345 Stockton Street
Tel. 415-398-1234

Hilton and Towers San Francisco
333 O'Farrell Street
Tel. 415-771-1400
No concierge

Ground Transport

It is possible to hail cabs on the street downtown, but not easy.
Renting a car is not wise due to parking difficulties.

Car Services: Capitol 415-752-5055
                  Corporate Choice 415-407-8914
                  Premiere 415-206-9999

Washington, D.C.

Overview

The District of Columbia is diamond-shaped and covers sixty-
eight square miles with 600,000 inhabitants. The District is sur-
rounded by a highway called the Beltway or the Loop. Imagine
the Capitol, the Mall, and the White House in the center, with
four quadrants surrounding them: Northwest, Northeast,
Southwest, and Southeast. These quadrants are important to
understand because they are used by everyone to give directions
(including the U.S. Postal Service and taxi drivers). Within the
quadrants are neighborhoods, and again, the names of these
neighborhoods are used when giving directions. The Northwest
quadrant includes Georgetown, Adams Morgan, and Dupont
Circle. The Northeast is The Hill (the neighborhood surrounding Capitol Hill); some areas on The Hill can be dangerous, particularly at night. The Southeast quadrant can also be very
dangerous. The Southwest quadrant includes major federal
buildings such as the IRS, the Justice Department, and the

Federal Trade Commission. People refer to Washington, D.C., simply as "D.C."

Airports

Reagan National Airport serves domestic travel only. It takes ten minutes to get from the airport to downtown by car.

Baltimore Washington International (BWI) serves all international travel. It is thirty miles from downtown D.C., and takes forty minutes to get to.

Dulles International Airport is twenty-six miles from downtown, and it takes twenty to forty minutes to get there.

Hotels

The Four Seasons
2800 Pennsylvania Avenue
Tel. 202-342-0444

The Hay Adams
1 Lafayette Square
Tel. 202-638-6600

Hyatt Regency
400 New Jersey Avenue, NW
Tel. 202-737-1234

The Willard
1401 Pennsylvania Avenue
Tel. 202-628-9100

The Jefferson
1200 16th Street, NW
Tel. 202-347-2200

Ground Transport

It is possible to hail taxis on the street in D.C.; however, there are a couple of things you and your boss need to know about cab service in the nation's capital. When you give a cab driver the address of where you want to go, you must also tell him the quadrant. Cabs can pick up more than one passenger along a route, making riding in a cab like carpooling with strangers. You can find yourself squeezed against a total stranger or two, and certainly not having any privacy for cell phone conversations. Cabs in D.C. are usually in really bad condition—torn seats, dirty, old, worn-out shocks, etc. Cab fares are based on zones not meters. By law, there are maps of zones in every cab, but it is a complicated system to understand as a visitor and you will not know if you are being cheated.

Car rental is probably a mistake due to lack of parking.

Car Services: Roadmaster 202-362-4335
                 Limo Scene 703-503-5466
                 Majestic 703-461-3700 or 301-840-2090

Boston

Overview

Boston has an unusual configuration because of its age and subsequent lack of urban planning. Beyond the downtown, neighborhoods are classified by the ethnicity of the majority of their residents. To the east of Boston Common the downtown area includes the financial and government centers. The Government Center is home to many historic landmarks. Charlestown and South Boston are Irish; East Boston and North End are Italian; Roxbury and Dorchester are African American; there are Chinatown and Latino neighborhoods, and the wealthy, mostly white, Beacon Hill and Back Bay. Back Bay is the location of Newbury Street, which is a renowned shopping street. Boston's main industry is education. There are forty universities in and around it. There is a thriving nightlife district on Lansdowne Street behind Fenway Park Stadium.

Airports
Logan International Airport is near the city center and it takes fifteen to twenty minutes to get there by car.

Hotels

Boston Park Plaza Hotel (1927 Landmark)
64 Arlington Street
Tel. 617-426-2000
Pool

The Fairmount Copley Plaza (1912 Landmark)
138 Saint James Avenue
Tel. 617-267-5300

The Ritz-Carlton (built in 1927, elegant)
15 Arlington Street
Tel. 617-536-5700

Hilton Back Bay
40 Dalton Street
Tel. 617-236-1100
Pool

Four Seasons Hotel
200 Boylston Street
Tel. 617-338-4400
Pool

Le Meridien
250 Franklin Street
Tel. 617-451-1900
Pool

Ground Transport
Boston's taxis have a bad reputation; they are often dirty, ineffi-
cient, and unreliable, and the drivers often do not speak
English. Besides, it is not possible to hail them on the streets.
Driving in Boston is not a good idea because finding parking is
very difficult and there is always a lot of construction.

Car Services: CEO Transportation 800-844-0696
                 Cambridge Limo 800-707-8306

Chicago

Overview
Chicago is a city of three million people, on Lake Michigan.
More than any other destination, it is important that you check
the weather before your boss travels to Chicago because the
wind off the lake can be brutal; yet spring can be mild and the
summers are hot. There are two central areas of Chicago, the
downtown and Lake Shore Drive (aka the Magnificent Mile).
There are beautiful hotels, shopping, and restaurants on Lake
Shore Drive just as there are downtown. As with Los Angeles,
the best advice is for your boss to stay near where his business
is. Many commercial ventures have relocated to the outlying
neighborhoods.

Airports
O'Hare International Airport is about twenty miles from
downtown (it competes with Atlanta's Hartsfield as the world's

busiest airport) and Midway Airport is only ten miles from downtown. Even though the airports are close to the city center, because of traffic it takes forty-five to sixty minutes to get there by car from either airport.

Hotels—Downtown

The Fairmont Hotel (one of the best hotels in Chicago)
200 North Columbus Drive
Tel. 312-565-8000
Pool

Sheraton Chicago Hotel and Towers
301 East North Water Street
Tel. 312-464-1000
Pool

Swissotel Chicago (modern European décor)
323 East Wacker Drive
Tel. 312-565-0565
Pool. Golf

Blackstone Hotel (landmark, built in 1910)
636 South Michigan Avenue
Tel. 312-427-4300

Hotel Burnham (landmark building)
1 West Washington
Tel. 312-782-1111

Hyatt Regency McCormick Place
2233 MLK Drive
Tel. 312-567-1234
Pool

Hyatt on Printers Row (Art Deco décor)
500 South Dearborn Street
Tel. 312-986-1234

Renaissance Chicago Hotel
One West Wacker Drive
Tel. 312-372-7200
Pool. Kinkos Copy Center on ground floor

Congress Plaza Hotel (built in 1893)
520 South Michigan Avenue
Tel. 312-427-3800

Palmer House Hilton (very elegant)
17 East Monroe Street
Tel. 312-726-7500
Pool

Tremont Hotel (small and European)
100 East Chestnut Street
Tel. 312-751-1900

Hilton and Towers Chicago
720 South Michigan Avenue
Tel. 312-922-4400
Pool

Hotels—Magnificent Mile Area

The Drake Hotel (built in 1920)
140 East Walton Place
Tel. 312-787-2200

Four Seasons Hotel
120 East Delaware Place
Tel. 312-280-8800
Pool

Ground Transport
Taxis are available to hail on the streets downtown, and there
are taxi stands outside the major hotels.

Car Services: Crown Cars 800-876-7725
                   Metro Limo 800-437-1700

Atlanta

Overview
The shape of modern Atlanta is formed by three highways;
imagine one running north-south, and another east-west. The
third highway is a ring around the city. The downtown center is
at the junction of the north-south and east-west highways; it
includes the Five Points neighborhood and the business and
historic districts. Immediately north of downtown is a neighborhood called Midtown, and three miles north of downtown
is Buckhead, which is a village unto itself. Buckhead is a
wealthy commercial and residential neighborhood with a
vibrant nightlife, which is referred to as the Beverly Hills of the
South. Peachtree is the main artery running through downtown and it is referred to as "P'tree." The population is 425,000
and the main industries are Coca-Cola and CNN.

Airports
Hartsfield International Airport alternates with Chicago's
O'Hare Airport as the busiest airport in the world. It is at the

southern tip of the city of Atlanta, ten miles south of downtown, and it takes fifteen minutes to get there.

Hotels

Ritz-Carlton Atlanta (very elegant, decorated with antiques
and Persian carpets)
181 Peachtree Street, NE
Tel. 404-659-0400

Atlanta Hilton and Towers NE
255 Courtland Street
Tel. 404-659-2000
Pool

Sheraton Atlanta Hotel
165 Courtland Street
Tel. 404-659-6500
Pool

The Westin Peachtree Plaza
210 Peachtree Street NW
Tel. 404-659-1400
Pool

Ground Transport

Taxis from the airport to downtown charge a flat fee. Taxis tend
to be expensive and the drivers erratic, but there are lots of them
available to hail on the streets downtown and in Buckhead.

Car Services: Atlanta Limo 888-667-9300
                  Winful Executive 770-473-1130
                  CAM Limo 404-762-0755

Dallas

Overview

Dallas is home to the third largest number of Fortune 500 companies in the United States, and probably only about 50 percent
of businesses are located downtown. One million people live in
Dallas, and half a million live in Forth Worth, immediately next
to Dallas. The city covers 9,000 square miles, and like Los
Angeles, the greater Dallas–Fort Worth metro area contains
multiple little townships. It has four times as many restaurants
per person than New York City; of course, many of these are in
malls because Dallas also has more shopping malls per capita
than any other U.S. city. There is shopping downtown at the
West End Marketplace and Downtown Underground (an
underground mall). Nightlife activity is clustered in West End,
Deep Ellum, and Lower Greenville. Dallas is very, very hot in the
summer. During one of their heat waves the temperature can be
115 degrees, and there is a cold wind in the winter.

Airports

Dallas–Fort Worth International Airport, one of the busiest
airports in the world, is eighteen miles northeast of downtown
immediately between Fort Worth and Dallas. Allow forty-five
minutes to travel from the airport to downtown.

Love Field is the hub of Southwest Airlines and is small and
downtown, actually near one of the wealthiest residential areas
of the city.

Hotels

The Aristocrat (built in 1925 by Conrad Hilton)
1933 Main Street
Tel. 214-741-7700

Hyatt Regency
300 Reunion Boulevard
Tel. 214-651-1234

The Mansion on Turtle Creek
2821 Turtle Creek Boulevard
Tel. 214-559-2100
Pool

The Magnolia
1401 Commerce Street
Tel. 214-915-6500

Ground Transport
Taxis are not available on the street, and because distances are
great the fares are large. Renting a car is inadvisable because the
streets are confusing and traffic is bad. However, if your boss is
driving himself, tell him that he should take toll roads whenever possible because they are notoriously less trafficked in
Texas than other highways.

Car Services: Executive Car Service 800-743-3151
                  Alberton Limousine 214-363-3149

Houston

Overview
Houston's population is 4.5 million, and it is a massive sprawling
city beyond the downtown area (the distance across the city is
approximately sixty miles). It is important that your boss stay in a
hotel near where his business is, otherwise he'll be wasting a lot of
time in a car. Houston is shaped like a wheel and all the major
thoroughfares are interstate highways. The spokes of the wheel are
interstates and there are multiple ring roads, which are also inter-

states. The downtown is the commercial and business district and it contains many restaurants and, of course, hotels. There are underground, air-conditioned tunnels and malls underneath the streets of the downtown. Houston has a second business district called the Galleria which is to the west of downtown. To the east of downtown are the petrochemical refineries, and unless your boss has specific business there, he shouldn't go there. There is a huge medical center just barely south of downtown, and the theater and concert district is to the north of downtown.

Houston has a tropical climate, with summer lasting from March through December and very high humidity for six months of the year.

Airports

George Bush Intercontinental Airport is forty minutes from downtown by car. Hobby Airport is a smaller airport, and therefore quicker to move through, but fewer flights come through. It is thirty minutes from downtown by car and in a questionable part of town—so don't book your boss into a hotel around Hobby Airport. Allow twenty extra minutes for any drive in the morning due to traffic.

Hotels

The Warwick (built in 1925)
5701 Main Street
Tel. 713-526-1991
Pool

Four Seasons Hotel
1300 Lamar Street
Tel. 713-650-1300
Pool

Hyatt Regency Downtown
1200 Lousiana Street
Tel. 713-654-1234
Pool

Ground Transport
Taxis on the street are almost nonexistent in Houston, so a visitor must have a car to get around because distances are so vast, and the climate is so unforgiving. The traffic is awful in Houston (like Los Angeles), so remember to add enough travel time between appointments on your boss's schedule. If your boss is driving, tell him to use the toll roads whenever possible because they have less traffic on them than the other interstate highways.

Car Services: Ace Limo 713-223-5466
                 Courtesy 713-520-1313
                 Signature Limousine 888-972-5466

Philadelphia

Overview
Philadelphia covers 129 square miles with 111 distinct neighborhoods. The metropolitan population is 5 million. However, the city center is clearly laid out and easy to navigate. City Hall is in the direct center of Philadelphia, literally. The downtown area around City Hall is called Center City, and is located between two rivers, the Delaware on the east and the Schuylkill on the west. Center City is bound on the north by Vine Street and on the south by Cedar Street. The streets are laid out on a grid with the north-south streets being numbered (except Broad Street) and the east-west streets named after trees

(except High Street and Market Street). Broad Street is the main artery running north-south through Center City, and it is also called Avenue of the Arts.

Airports
Philadelphia International Airport is fifteen to thirty minutes from downtown.

Hotels

The Ritz-Carlton (landmark)
10 Avenue of the Arts
Tel. 215-735-7700

Park Hyatt at the Bellevue
Broad and Walnut streets
Tel. 215-893-1776

Sheraton Society Hill
I Dock Street
Tel. 215-238-6000
No laundry service. No concierge

Ground Transport
It is possible to hail taxis downtown.

Car Service: Academy 215-333-3333

Miami

Overview
Miami has a population of 2 million, with 700,000 being the Cuban community. Miami is split into quadrants which meet at the junction of Miami Avenue and Flagler Street. Avenues

and courts run north and south; streets, ways, and terraces run east and west; and roads run diagonally. Little Havana is to the east of downtown, Coconut Grove is to the southeast, and Coral Gables, the location of the University of Miami, is to the south. Across the Intercoastal Waterway on a barrier island is Miami Beach.

Airports
Miami International Airport is fifteen to twenty minutes from downtown Miami.

Hotels—Downtown

Hyatt Regency
400 SE 2nd Avenue
Tel. 305-358-1234
Pool

Sheraton Biscayne Bay
495 Brickell Avenue
Tel. 305-373-6000
No laundry service. No concierge

Hotels—Miami Beach

Fontainebleau Hilton Resort and Towers
4441 Collins Avenue
Tel. 315-538-2000
Pool

Eden Roc Resort and Spa
4525 Collins Avenue
Tel. 305-531-0000
Pool

Beach House Bal Harbour
9449 Collins Avenue
Tel. 305-865-3551
Pool

Ground Transport
There are no taxis on the streets to hail and even if they are called and booked ahead they are notoriously dangerous.

Car Services: ABC Limo 800-380-1222
                   Status Limo 305-638-2989

Tampa

Overview
Tampa Bay is a body of water and an area comprised of three cities: Tampa, St. Petersburg, Clearwater, and many small beach towns and residential communities. The population of Tampa Bay is 2.5 million. Tampa is the commercial center of Southwest Florida. Ybor City is located within Tampa and is the historic Cuban district, where the cigar-making industry started. It's now the location of a vibrant night scene.

Airports
Tampa International Airport is ten minutes by car from downtown Tampa.

Hotels

Hyatt Regency
211 North Tampa Street
Tel. 727-225-1234

Ground Transport
Taxis are not available on the streets in Tampa, and driving is difficult because the streets are not well marked.

Car Service: AAA Limo 877-507-LIMO

Denver

Overview
Denver covers 155 square miles and has a population of half a million, with eighty distinct neighborhoods. It's a sprawling western city. The main industries are cable television, telecommunications, and computer software. The center of Denver is the Civic Center, which is located over three city blocks, and at one end of it is the State Capitol. The downtown area around the Civic Center contains the Convention Center and the 16th Street Mall, which is a pedestrian area of shops and restaurants. Cherry Creek runs diagonally to the west of the Civic Center. LoDo, which stands for Lower Downtown, is located to the northwest of the Civic Center and is a renovated historic district with a vibrant nightlife. There are over three-hundred days of sunshine per year in Denver—remind your boss to take her sunglasses. The cities of Golden and Boulder are attached to Denver on the west side of the city.

Airports
Denver International Airport is the world's largest airport, and the sixth busiest airport in America. It takes about forty-five minutes to get from the airport to downtown.

Hotels

The Brown Palace (historic)
321 17th Street
Tel. 303-297-3111

Hyatt Regency
1750 Welton Street
Tel. 303-295-1234
Pool

Marriott City Center
1701 California Street
Tel. 303-297-1300
Pool. No laundry service

Adam's Mark Hotel
1550 Court Place
Tel. 303-893-3333
No concierge

Ground Transport
Taxis are available only at hotels.

Car Services: Presidential Limousine 800-442-5422
                  White Dove Limo 303-399-3683

Indianapolis

Overview
The center of Indianapolis is Monument Circle, a 280-foot
spire from which all the main avenues of the city radiate. The
original downtown is one square mile and the streets are numbered. The downtown is renovated and there is a new stadium

and the City Market, Union Station, and Canal Walk, which are all commercial areas of shops and restaurants. One of the main industries of Indianapolis is sports, in particular, auto racing. The Indianapolis 500 occurs every May, and festivals and preparations begin for the entire month before. In the summer it's hot and in the winter it's cold. On the northwest side of the city there is a 4,200-acre city park called Eagle Creek Park.

Airports
Indianapolis International Airport is ten to fifteen minutes from downtown by car.

Hotels

Canterbury Hotel (historic)
123 S. Illinois Street
Tel. 317-634-3000
No room service. No concierge

Omni Severin Hotel
40 West Jackson Place
Tel. 317-634-6664
Pool

Crowne Plaza Union Station
123 West Louisiana
Tel. 317-631-2221
Pool. No room service. No concierge

Courtyard by Marriott
320 North Senate Avenue
Tel. 317-684-7733
Pool. No room service. No concierge

Ground Transport

It is possible to get around the downtown area on foot, and taxis are available on the street.

Car Services: Hoosier Limousine 888-248-8879
                 Carey Indiana 800-888-INDY

Cincinnati

Overview

Cincinnati is the leading pork packer in the world, so you'll notice a lot of references to pigs in the names of things as you plan a trip here. The city is built on a series of hills in the basin of the Ohio River. The center of the city is Fountain Square in the thriving downtown which contains lots of restaurants and shopping. The city is split between the East and West sides. The West Side is more traditional and working class; the East Side is more trendy, young, and upwardly mobile. Streets running east and west are numbered and those running north and south have names. Because it's located in the basin of the river, the city is hot and humid in the summer.

Airports

Cincinnati/Northern Kentucky International Airport is thirteen miles from downtown Cincinnati, and it takes about thirty minutes to get there by car.

Hotels

Omni Netherland Plaza (historic)
35 W. 5th Street
Tel. 513-421-9100
Pool

The Cincinnatian Hotel
601 Vine Street
Tel. 513-381-3000

Hyatt Regency
151 West 5th Street
Tel. 513-579-1234

Radisson
11320 Chester Road
Tel. 513-772-1720

Ground Transport
There is a taxi stand in the center of downtown at Fountain
Square.

Car Services: Johnny Miller Limousines 812-926-2222 or
                   800-355-4668
                 M&M Limos 888-545-4693 or 513-598-5530
                 Starz Limo 513-942-0836

Cleveland

Overview
Cleveland hugs Lake Erie. The geographic center of the city is
Terminal Tower, which is an office and shopping complex. The
lake is northwest of Terminal Tower. There are two sports stadi-
ums downtown, and the Rock and Roll Hall of Fame is north
of downtown. Fifteen minutes to the east of downtown is
University Circle, which is home to many cultural institutions.
When visiting, you'll want to stay on the east side of town
(Note: The far east side is suburbs). The downtown area is well
developed with a former industrial waterfront area known as

The Flats, which has lots of great restaurants. Around the stadiums is the Warehouse District, which has a vibrant nightlife.

Airports
Cleveland Hopkins International Airport is twenty to thirty minutes from downtown.

Hotels

The Ritz-Carlton
1515 West 3rd Street
Tel. 216-623-1300
Pool

Renaissance Cleveland Hotel
24 Public Square
Tel. 216-696-5600
Pool. No laundry service. No concierge

Marriott at Key Center
127 Public Square
Tel. 216-696-9200
No laundry service. No room service

Ground Transport
Taxis are not available on the streets of Cleveland; it is very spread out, so a car is essential to get around anywhere but the Waterfront area downtown.

Car Services: Hopkins Airport Limo 800-543-9912
                 Renaissance Limo 888-796-5466
                 J&F Luxury 216-447-1111

Detroit

Overview

Detroit is built on the Detroit River. The Renaissance Center (known as the "Ren Cen") is right on the riverfront and is a massive commercial complex of six office towers and over ninety shops and restaurants. It's the focal point of downtown Detroit and is a city within a city. The headquarters for General Motors is located in the Ren Cen. Next to the Ren Cen is the Civic Center, which is a seventy-five-acre area on the riverfront for cultural and sports activities. North of the Ren Cen is the Grand Circus, which is the original center of Detroit, and all the streets radiate out from it. Greektown is to the southeast and is the main entertainment district of the city. South of downtown is Bricktown, which is a renovated industrial area and home to many restaurants and nightclubs. The university and museums are north of downtown, and to the east is Rivertown, which is made up of refurbished factories and now houses nightclubs and restaurants. West of downtown are the Latino neighborhoods.

Airports

Wayne County Detroit Metro Airport (DTW) is twenty to twenty-five minutes by car from downtown.

Hotels

Hotel Pontchartrain
2 Washington Boulevard
Tel. 313-965-0200
No laundry service

Courtyard by Marriott
333 East Jefferson Avenue
Tel. 313-222-7700
No laundry service. No concierge

Ground Transport

Taxis in Detroit are known to be in bad condition and unreliable. They aren't available on the streets.

Car Services: AA Premiere Limo 313-345-3880
                    Ashton Limo 313-925-0260
                    Enterprise Limo 313-934-3383
                    Masters 313-861-6132
                    Luxury Sedan 313-331-1211
                    Fairchild Limousines 877-836-5466

Austin

Overview

There is a loop highway around Austin (I360) and a highway that runs north-south down the east side of the city (I35). Congress Avenue runs right through downtown, and at its north end is the Capitol building. Sixth Street, and the Warehouse district (4th and 5th Streets), famous for nightclubs with live music, are downtown. The University of Texas is north of downtown (the main street through campus is Guadalupe, aka the Drag); immediately south of downtown is Town Lake. Further south is Zilker Park, which contains a swimming hole of spring-fed water called Barton Springs. East of downtown is a mostly Hispanic neighborhood which can be dangerous, particularly at night. The high-tech industry in Austin is located north and west of downtown off Anderson Lane. To the far west of downtown is a wealthy residential neighborhood. It's likely that your boss's business will not be in downtown Austin, but he can get anywhere by car in about fifteen to twenty minutes.

Airports

Austin Bergstrom International Airport is ten to fifteen minutes from downtown by car.

Hotels

Four Seasons Hotel
98 San Jacinto Boulevard
Tel. 512-478-4500
Pool

Omni
700 San Jacinto
Tel. 512-476-3700
No room service. No laundry service

Hyatt Regency
208 Barton Springs Road
Tel. 512-477-1234
No room service. No concierge. No laundry service

Ground Transport

In fifteen minutes you can get anywhere in Austin. There are no taxis on the streets in Austin.

Car Services: Ace Limousine 512-926-5466
                  Austin Area Limousine 512-386-8600 or
                  800-767-4090

New Orleans

Overview

New Orleans is located on the Mississippi River and its climate is tropical. The three main areas of the city form a triangle: the French Quarter, the Garden District, and the CBD (Central Business District). It's a small city and your boss can stay in any one of these areas no matter where his business is. The main industry of New Orleans is tourism and conventions, so the city is well equipped for a traveler; for example, there are taxis available on the streets. There are some dangerous areas of the French Quarter and if your boss is easily offended, you should let him know that it can be pretty wild at night down there.

Airports

The New Orleans International Airport is in Kenner, about fourteen miles northwest of New Orleans, and it takes twenty to thirty minutes to get to the CBD.

Hotels

Fairmount (historic)
University Place
Tel. 504-529-7111
Pool. Tennis courts

Windsor Court
300 Gravier Street
Tel. 504-523-6000
Pool

Omni Royal Orleans Hotel
621 St. Louis Street
Tel. 504-529-5333
Pool

Ground Transportation
There are taxis to hail on the streets in the French Quarter and
the CBD.

Car Services: London Livery Ltd. 504-586-0700
                  Flagship Limousine 504-486-4562

index

Printed in the United States
46524LVS00005B/100-117